C000242496

ORIGAMI
STARS

Other books by John Montroll
www.johnmontroll.com

General Origami

Origami Worldwide
Teach Yourself Origami: Second Revised Edition
Christmas Origami
Storytime Origami

Animal Origami

Dragons and Other Fantastic Creatures in Origami
Bugs in Origami
Horses in Origami
Origami Birds
Origami Gone Wild
Dinosaur Origami
Origami Dinosaurs for Beginners
Mythological Creatures and the Chinese Zodiac Origami
Origami Under the Sea
Sea Creatures in Origami
Origami for the Enthusiast
Animal Origami for the Enthusiast

Geometric Origami

Origami and Math: Simple to Complex
Classic Polyhedra Origami
A Constellation of Origami Polyhedra
Galaxy of Origami Stars

Dollar Bill Origami

Dollar Bill Animals in Origami
Dollar Bill Origami
Easy Dollar Bill Origami

Simple Origami

Easy Origami Animals
Fun and Simple Origami: 101 Easy-to-Fold Projects
Super Simple Origami
Easy Dollar Bill Origami
Easy Origami

ORIGAMI STARS

JOHN MONTROLL

WITH CONTRIBUTIONS BY
RUSSELL CASHDOLLAR

DOVER PUBLICATIONS, INC.
NEW YORK

To Sarah and Elliott

Bibliographical Note

Origami Stars is a new work, first published by
Dover Publications, Inc., in 2014.

Library of Congress Cataloging-in-Publication Data

Montroll, John.
 Origami stars / John Montroll.
   pages cm
 ISBN 978-0-486-77987-4 (alk. paper)
 ISBN 0-486-77987-4 (alk. paper)
 1. Origami. 2. Stars in art. I. Title.
 TT872.5.M67 2014
 736'.982–dc23

2014
2014020047

Manufactured in the United States by Courier Corporation
77987401   2014
www.doverpublications.com

Introduction

Origami stars are fun to fold and display. In this collection of forty two-dimensional stars, each folded from a single square sheet of paper, you will find colorful patterns with varying shapes and numbers of points, some even resembling pinwheels and propellers.

This full color book contains photos of all the stars along with fanciful scenes. These imaginative stars include Woven, Radiant, and Kaleidoscopic varieties. Models range from simple to low-complex. Most are my designs and some are designed by Russell Cashdollar. An ongoing story adds fun to the folding experience.

My first book of stars, *Galaxy of Origami Stars*, was well received and inspired this collection. For those interested in models with more geometric patterns, there are three-dimensional stars in *A Constellation of Origami Polyhedra*, and further three-dimensional shapes in my other polyhedra books.

The diagrams are drawn in the internationally approved Randlett-Yoshizawa style, which is easy to follow once you learn the basic folds. You can use any kind of square paper for these models, but the best results will be achieved with standard origami paper, which is colored on one side and white on the other (in the diagrams in this book, the shading represents the colored side). Duo origami paper, which has a different color on each side, is ideal for several of these star models and gives impressive results. Large sheets are easier to use than small ones.

Origami supplies can be found in arts and craft shops, or at Dover Publications online: www.doverpublications.com. You can also visit OrigamiUSA at www.origamiusa.org for origami supplies and other related information including an extensive list of local, national, and international origami groups.

I thank Russell Cashdollar for his contributions to this book, which include the Four-Pointed Magic Star and Colorful Shuriken. I thank Constantin Miranda for photographing several models and I also thank my editor, Charley Montroll.

John Montroll
www.johnmontroll.com

Contents

Symbols 9
Basic Folds 10
Appreciating Stars 12
Stars with 3 Points 13
Stars with 4 Points 19
Stars with 5 Points 41
Stars with 6 Points 56
Stars with 7 Points 89
Stars with 8 Points 93
Stars with More Points 116

★   Simple
★★ Intermediate
★★★ Complex

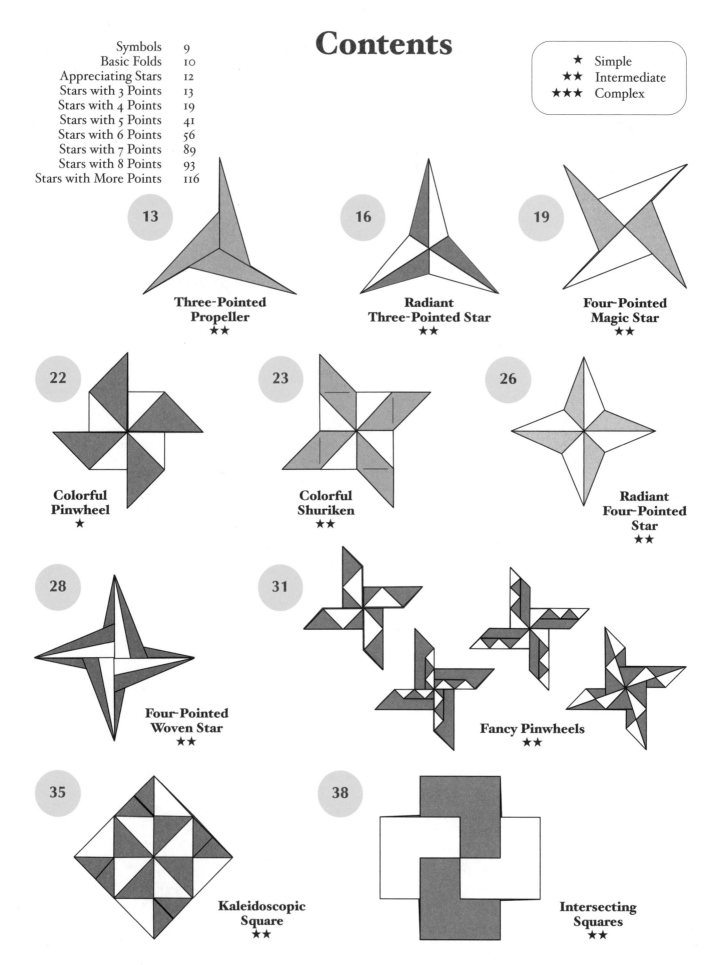

13

**Three-Pointed
Propeller**
★★

16

**Radiant
Three-Pointed Star**
★★

19

**Four-Pointed
Magic Star**
★★

22

**Colorful
Pinwheel**
★

23

**Colorful
Shuriken**
★★

26

**Radiant
Four-Pointed
Star**
★★

28

**Four-Pointed
Woven Star**
★★

31

Fancy Pinwheels
★★

35

**Kaleidoscopic
Square**
★★

38

**Intersecting
Squares**
★★

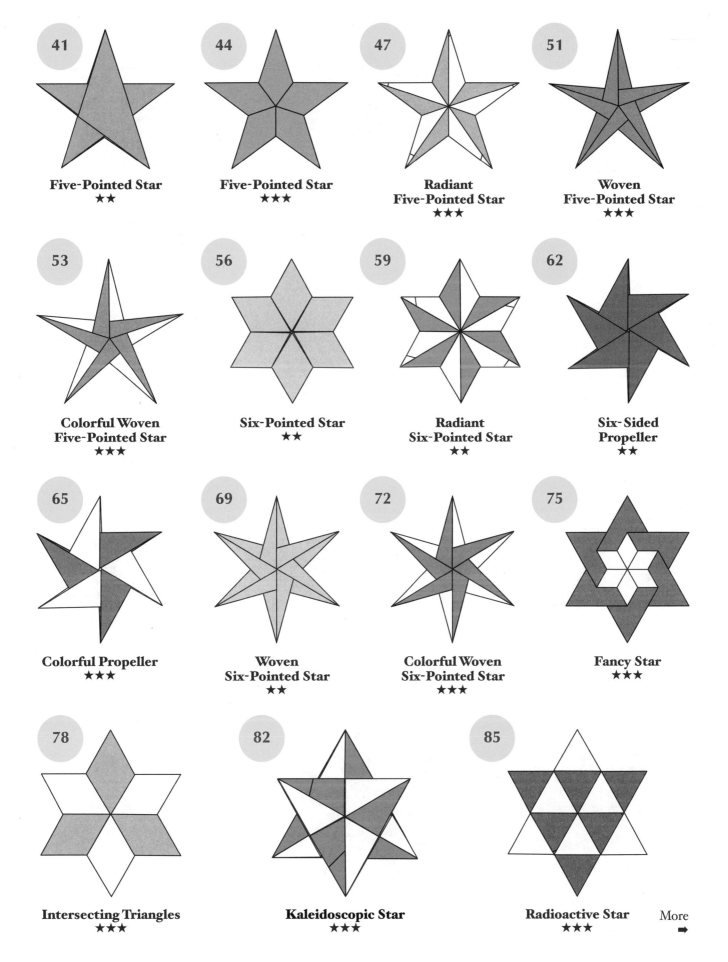

41

Five-Pointed Star
★★

44

Five-Pointed Star
★★★

47

**Radiant
Five-Pointed Star**
★★★

51

**Woven
Five-Pointed Star**
★★★

53

**Colorful Woven
Five-Pointed Star**
★★★

56

Six-Pointed Star
★★

59

**Radiant
Six-Pointed Star**
★★

62

**Six-Sided
Propeller**
★★

65

Colorful Propeller
★★★

69

**Woven
Six-Pointed Star**
★★

72

**Colorful Woven
Six-Pointed Star**
★★★

75

Fancy Star
★★★

78

Intersecting Triangles
★★★

82

Kaleidoscopic Star
★★★

85

Radioactive Star
★★★

More
➡

Contents 7

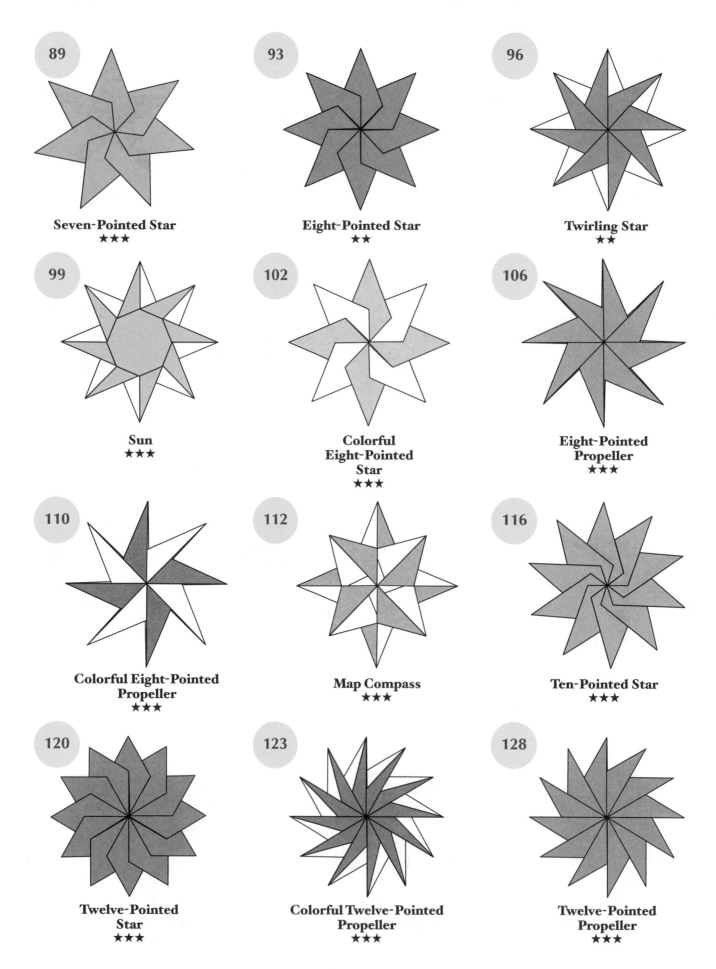

89 Seven-Pointed Star
★★★

93 Eight-Pointed Star
★★

96 Twirling Star
★★

99 Sun
★★★

102 Colorful
Eight-Pointed
Star
★★★

106 Eight-Pointed
Propeller
★★★

110 Colorful Eight-Pointed
Propeller
★★★

112 Map Compass
★★★

116 Ten-Pointed Star
★★★

120 Twelve-Pointed
Star
★★★

123 Colorful Twelve-Pointed
Propeller
★★★

128 Twelve-Pointed
Propeller
★★★

Symbols

Lines

— — — — — — — — —   Valley fold, fold in front.

— · · — · · — · · — · · — · · —   Mountain fold, fold behind.

————————————   Crease line.

···   X-ray or guide line.

Arrows

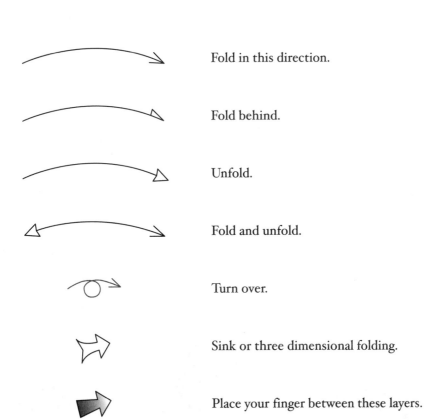

Fold in this direction.

Fold behind.

Unfold.

Fold and unfold.

Turn over.

Sink or three dimensional folding.

Place your finger between these layers.

Basic Folds

Pleat Fold.

Fold back and forth. Each pleat is composed of one valley and mountain fold. Here are two examples.

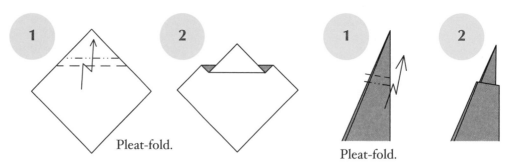

Pleat-fold.

Pleat-fold.

Squash Fold.

In a squash fold, some paper is opened and then made flat. The shaded arrow shows where to place your finger.

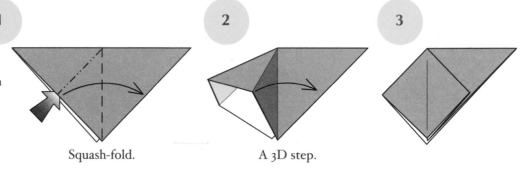

Squash-fold.

A 3D step.

Petal Fold.

In a petal fold, one point is folded up while two opposite sides meet each other.

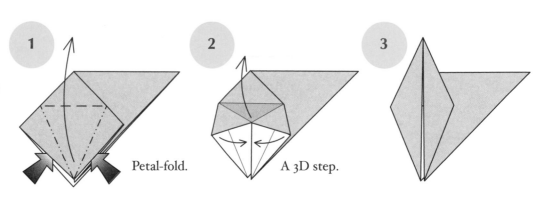

Petal-fold.

A 3D step.

Inside Reverse Fold.

In an inside reverse fold, some paper is folded between layers. Here are two examples.

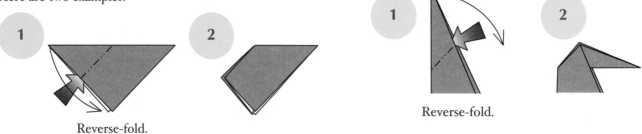

Reverse-fold.

Reverse-fold.

Waterbomb Base.

The waterbomb base is named for the waterbomb balloon which is made from it.

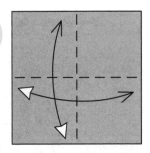

Fold and unfold.

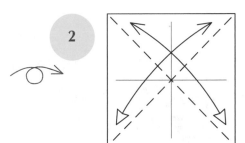

Fold and unfold.

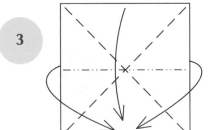

Collapse along the creases.

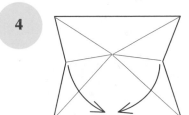

A 3D intermediate step.

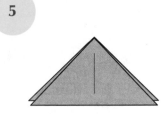

Waterbomb Base

Sink.

For a sink, some of the paper without edges is folded inside. To do this fold, much of the model must be unfolded.

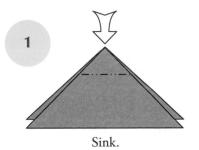

Sink.

Spread Squash Fold.

A cross between a squash fold and sink fold, some paper in the center is spread apart and then made flat.

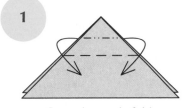

Spread-squash-fold.

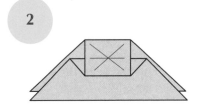

Appreciating Stars

Stars fill our world with wonder and mystery. One bright star shines through day, giving us light, heat, and so much more. At night that star disappears and the sky fills with tiny dots of distant, twinkling stars.

Ancient cultures saw the patterns of stars as part of the backdrop to an understanding of the world. What they noticed was that particular stars or constellations preceded seasons and thus these tiny dots of light could be used to predict life events. Voyagers who traveled the seas found that they could navigate by the stars, leading to greater and greater discoveries. Great minds, telescopes, and emerging technologies allowed people to break free of many misconceptions about the stars. Now we know more of the immense size, composition, and distance of stars. Learning about our place in the Milky Way, studying further galaxies, considering the nature and age of the universe and how and when the Big Bang might have occurred, and now the discovery of distant planets give us a deeper appreciation of everything, with yet more unsolved mysteries. Lest we humans believe we are the

only creatures who have made use of the stars, it has been found that the Scarab Beetle actually navigates at night by the Milky Way itself.

As the atmosphere gives stars the illusion of twinkling, throughout history, drawings depicting these celestial bodies have often been shown as being pointy, leading to interesting geometry. The drawings, originally shown to symbolize the stars above, took on new meaning as fanciful shapes, used for happy events. Two-dimensional representations appear in art from many cultures. Stars have become internationally-recognized symbols for awards and have been used as icons of power.

Folding stars gives us a new, personal enjoyment of these shapes. With interesting patterns and color changes, the sky is indeed the limit. It took history huge leaps of understanding to realize their significance and the vastness of our universe; on some distant planet in a far away galaxy, one wonders what stars might be folded by those inhabitants?

Stars with Three Points

The universe is full of countless stars in all varieties. We begin this cosmic journey by capturing three-pointed stars, formed in the distant past. Deep in space are two such stars, one has three thin points with a spiral effect and the other has a radiant alternating color pattern. Both stars use triangular symmetry which is easy to achieve from a square.

Your goal is to become the Master of the Universe by capturing all the stars and arranging them in cosmic harmony.

Three-Pointed Propeller

Designed by Russell Cashdollar

This Three-Pointed Propeller has triangular symmetry. The largest possible triangle from a square is shown in step 7. The triangle collapses into a smaller triangle in step 16 to allow for the thin points. Collapsing along the creases is a common theme in star formation. This is due to the immense gravity in its center.

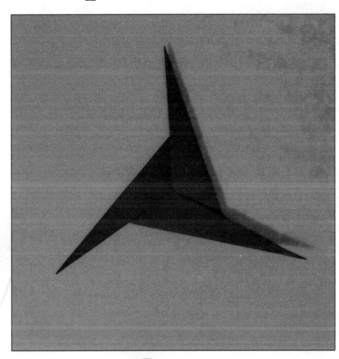

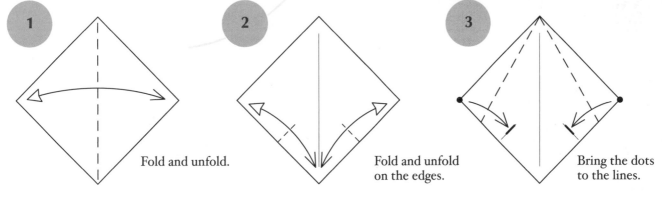

1 Fold and unfold.

2 Fold and unfold on the edges.

3 Bring the dots to the lines.

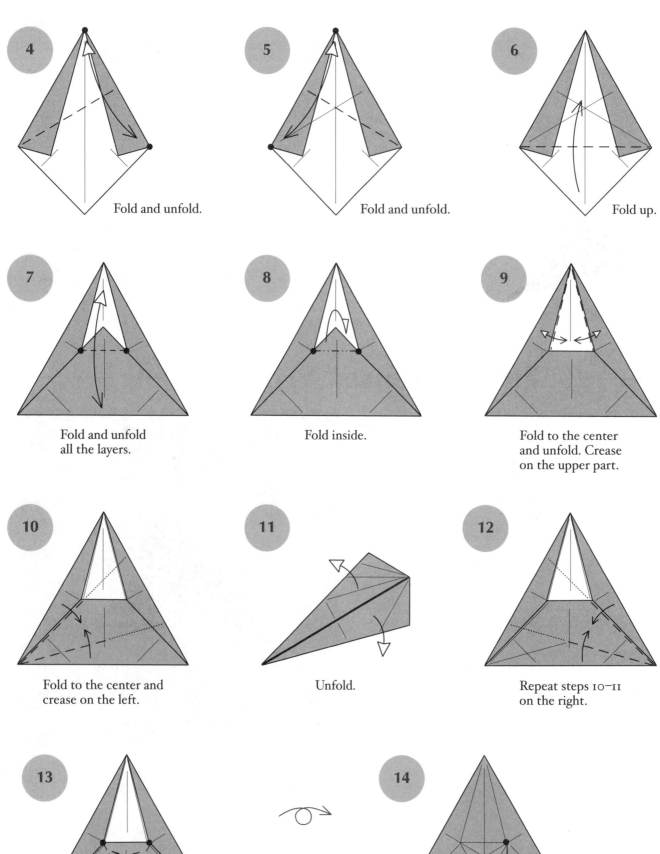

4 Fold and unfold.

5 Fold and unfold.

6 Fold up.

7 Fold and unfold all the layers.

8 Fold inside.

9 Fold to the center and unfold. Crease on the upper part.

10 Fold to the center and crease on the left.

11 Unfold.

12 Repeat steps 10–11 on the right.

13 Fold and unfold.

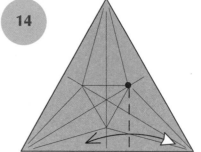

14 Fold and unfold. Rotate.

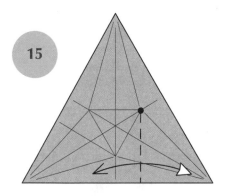

15

Repeat step 14
two times.

16

Collapse along the creases to
form a smaller triangle. The
dots will meet in the center.

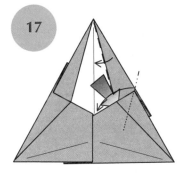

17

Reverse-fold. Rotate.

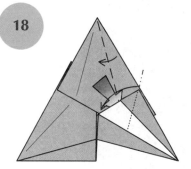

18

Repeat step 17
two times.

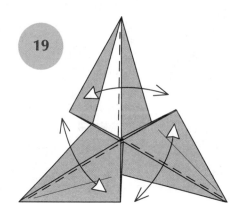

19

Fold and unfold.

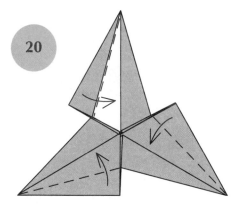

20

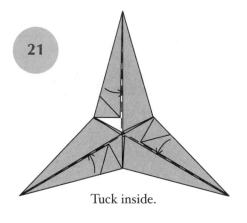

21

Tuck inside.

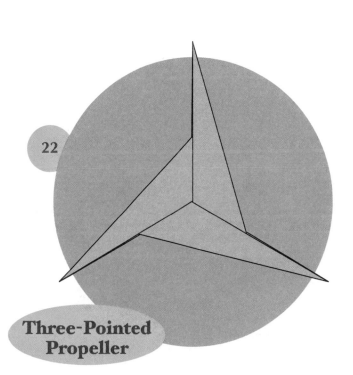

22

**Three-Pointed
Propeller**

Three-Pointed Propeller 15

Radiant Three-Pointed Star

Designed by Russell Cashdollar,
modified by John Montroll

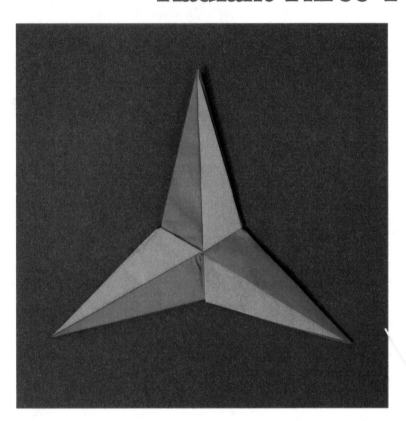

This star design was originally Russell Cashdollar's masterpiece. The folding process has been simplified by using book-fold symmetry, and much of the folding is similar to the previous star. Color effects add magic to this pulsating star.

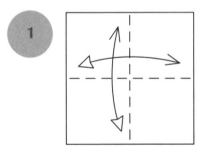

1 Fold and unfold.

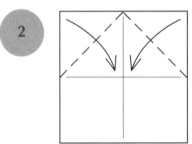

2 Fold to the center.

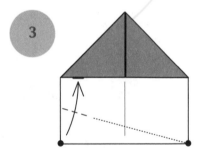

3 Bring the corner to the line. Crease on the left.

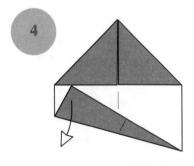

4 Unfold.

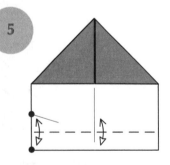

5 Fold and unfold so the dots meet on the left.

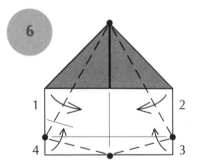

6 Fold in order.

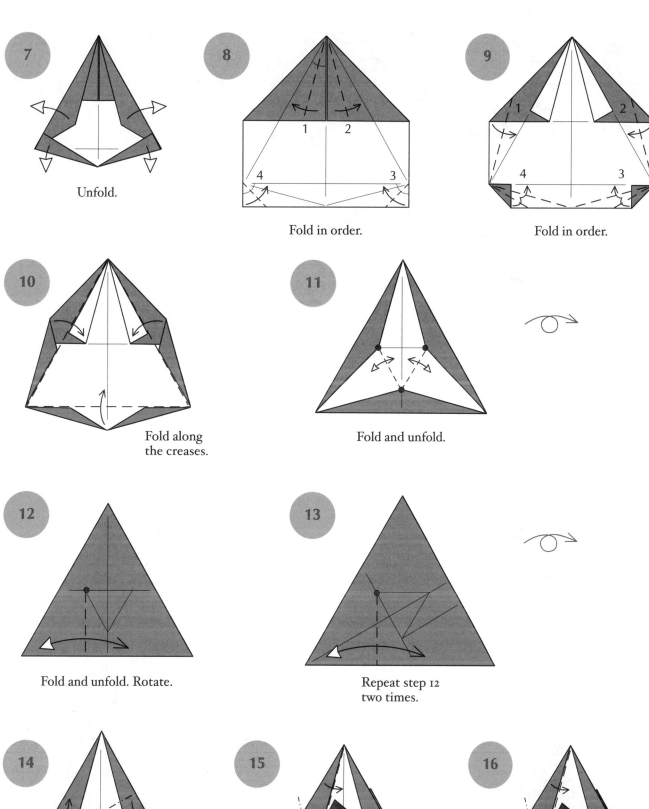

7 Unfold.

8 Fold in order.

9 Fold in order.

10 Fold along the creases.

11 Fold and unfold.

12 Fold and unfold. Rotate.

13 Repeat step 12 two times.

14 Collapse along the creases to form a smaller triangle.

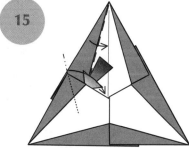

15 Reverse-fold. Rotate.

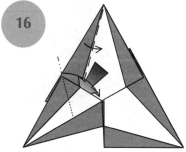

16 Repeat step 15 two times.

Bright and Shiny Stars

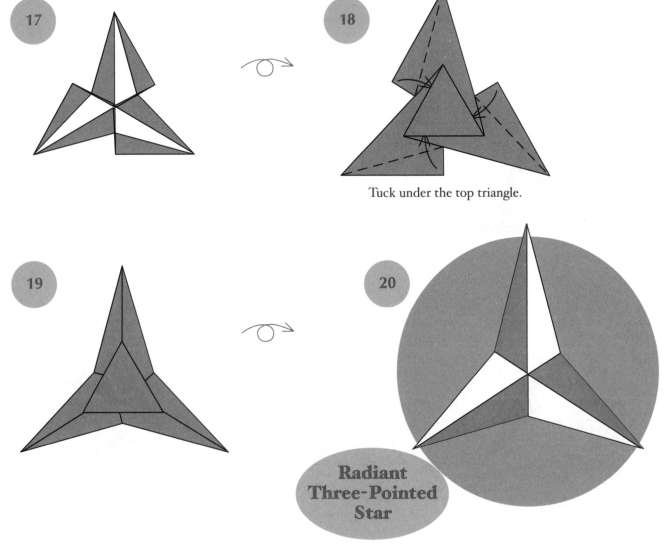

17

18

Tuck under the top triangle.

19

20

Radiant Three-Pointed Star

Stars with Four Points

The universe is teeming with four-pointed stars. No matter where stars have been observed, most have four points. Analysis has revealed that, as all stars begin with a square, their atomic structure shows high stability in four points. Thus only the brightest and rarest are shown here. All the four-pointed stars in this collection have colorful patterns and each can be captured in under 30 steps. The colors show their radiant energy while the fewer steps show their inherent stability and simplicity.

It is time to reach out and discover these celestial wonders to become Master of the four-pointed stars.

Four-Pointed Magic Star

Designed by Russell Cashdollar

This magic star is a rare find. Its brilliant alternating pattern on both sides makes it stand out, and it is also the largest star in the entire collection. Unusual folds, such as steps 15 through 21, reveal its central structure, the radiant source of its magic.

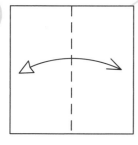

1

Fold and unfold.

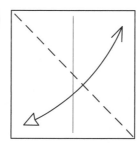

2

Fold and unfold.

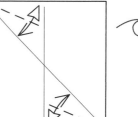

3

Fold and unfold.

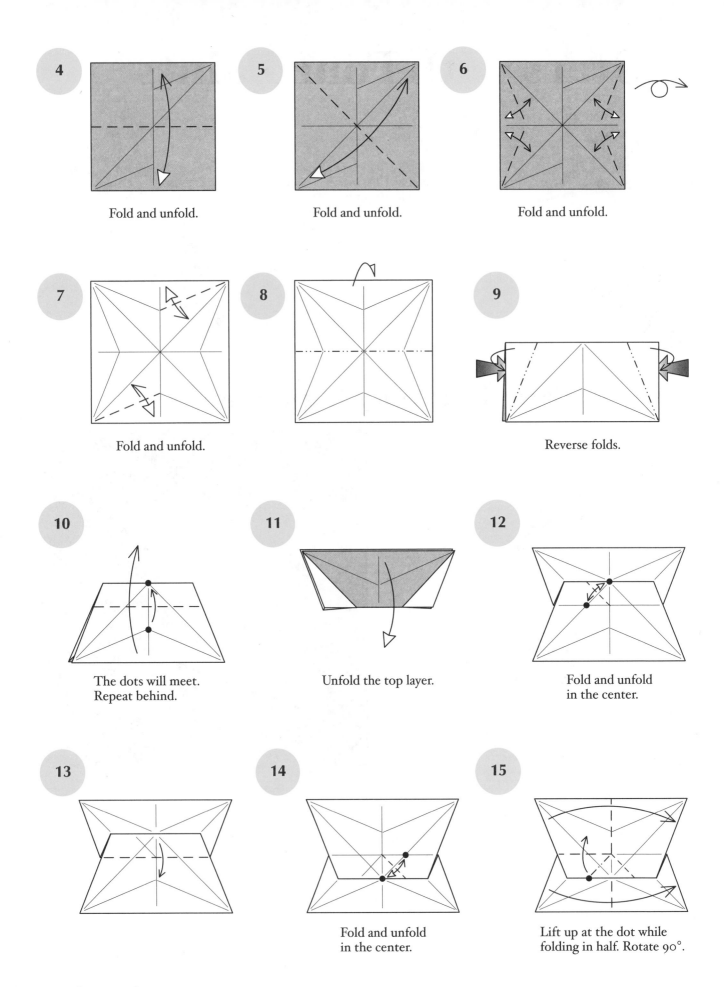

4 Fold and unfold.

5 Fold and unfold.

6 Fold and unfold.

7 Fold and unfold.

8

9 Reverse folds.

10 The dots will meet. Repeat behind.

11 Unfold the top layer.

12 Fold and unfold in the center.

13

14 Fold and unfold in the center.

15 Lift up at the dot while folding in half. Rotate 90°.

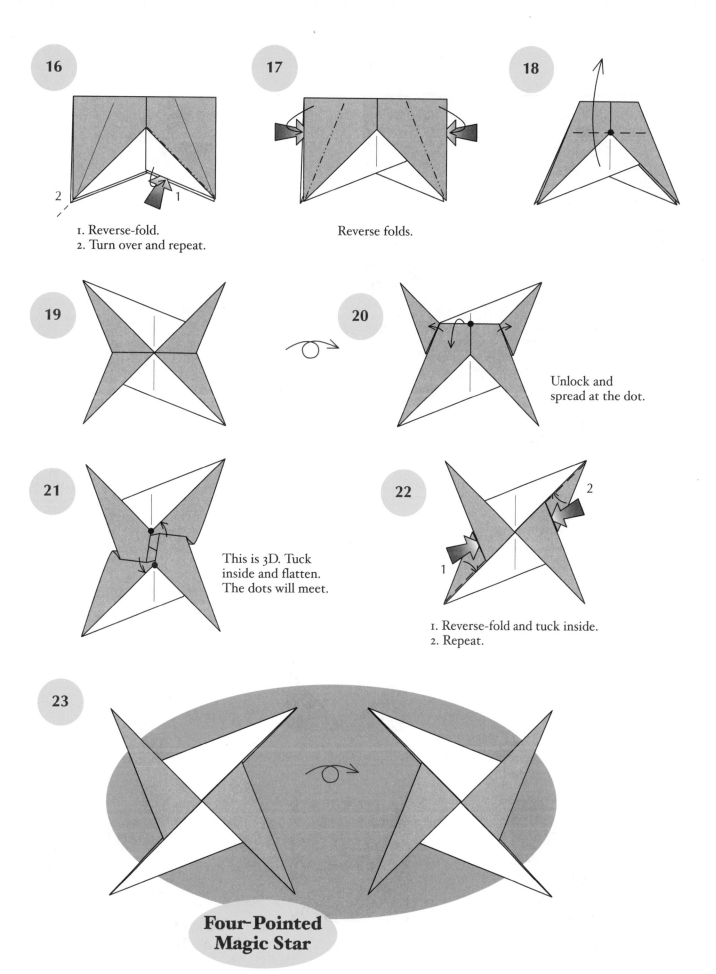

16

1. Reverse-fold.
2. Turn over and repeat.

17

Reverse folds.

18

19

20

Unlock and
spread at the dot.

21

This is 3D. Tuck
inside and flatten.
The dots will meet.

22

1. Reverse-fold and tuck inside.
2. Repeat.

23

**Four-Pointed
Magic Star**

Colorful Pinwheel

This colorful pinwheel is the simplest star in this collection. With one simple collapse in step 8, this spinning star is revealed.

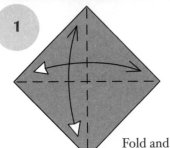

1 Fold and unfold.

2 Fold and unfold.

3 Fold to the center.

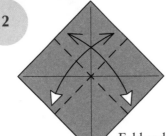

4 Fold from the center to the edges.

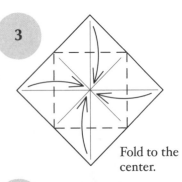

5 Fold to the center and unfold.

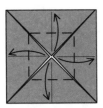

6 Fold and unfold in the center. Rotate 90°.

7 Repeat step 6 three times.

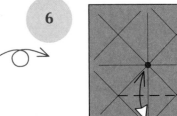

8 Collapse along the creases.

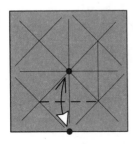

9 **Colorful Pinwheel**

Colorful Shuriken

Designed by Russell Cashdollar

T h e
first origami Shuriken was the
famous model made by folding two strips
of paper and interlocking them. Progressing
forward in time as the universe expanded, this
particular Shuriken was found to be created from
one square with a radiant colorful pattern. Now
it can also be folded with colors reversed
for another colorful effect.

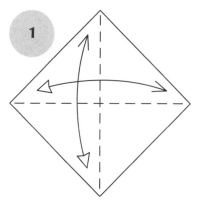

1 Fold and unfold.

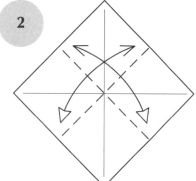

2 Fold and unfold.

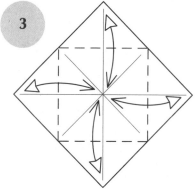

3 Fold to the center and unfold.

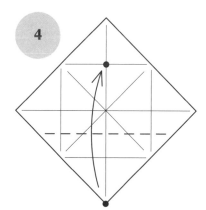

4 The dots will meet.

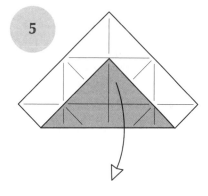

5 Unfold and rotate 90°.

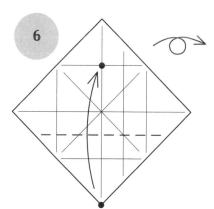

6 Repeat steps 4–5 three times.

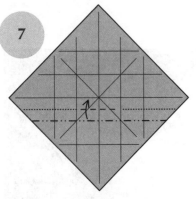

7

Pleat-fold to the center.
Mountain-fold along the crease.
Valley-fold in the center.

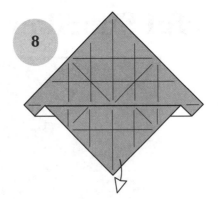

8

Unfold and rotate 90°.

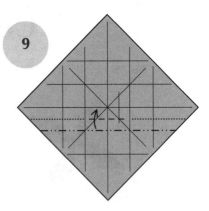

9

Repeat steps 7–8
three times.

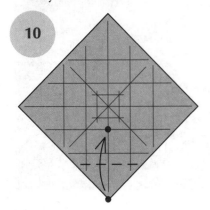

10

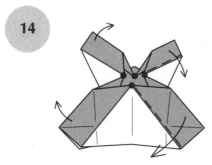

11

Fold and unfold.
Rotate 90°.

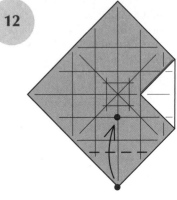

12

Repeat steps 10–11
three times.

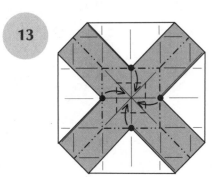

13

Collapse along the creases so
the four dots meet in the center.
This is similar to two sink folds.

14

This is 3D. Spiral and
flatten. The dots will meet.

15

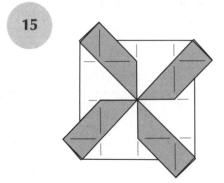

16

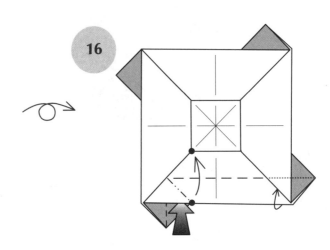

Squash-fold and
tuck inside on
the right.

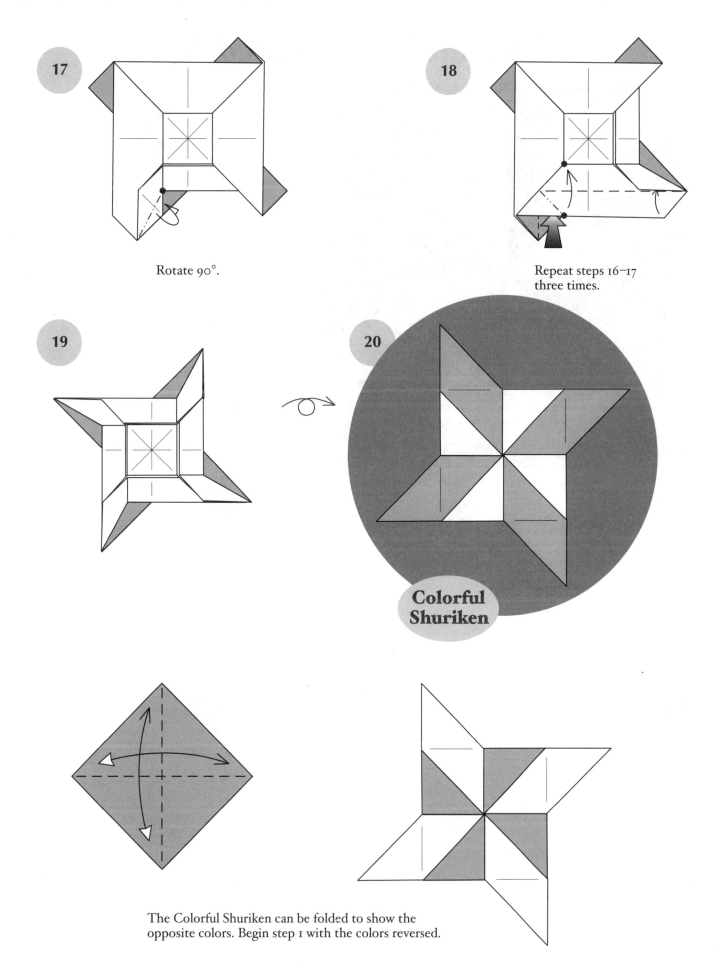

17

Rotate 90°.

18

Repeat steps 16–17 three times.

19

20

Colorful Shuriken

The Colorful Shuriken can be folded to show the opposite colors. Begin step 1 with the colors reversed.

Radiant Four-Pointed Star

This double-sided radiant star uses a twist fold from steps 9 to 12. Other radiant stars in this collection include the three, five and six-pointed stars.

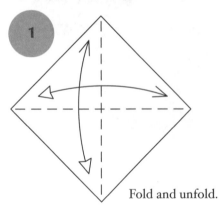

1 Fold and unfold.

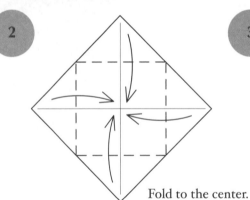

2 Fold to the center.

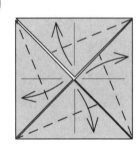

3

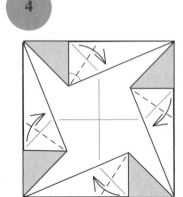

4

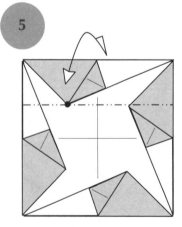

5 Fold and unfold.

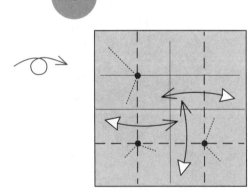

6 Fold and unfold by hidden landmarks.

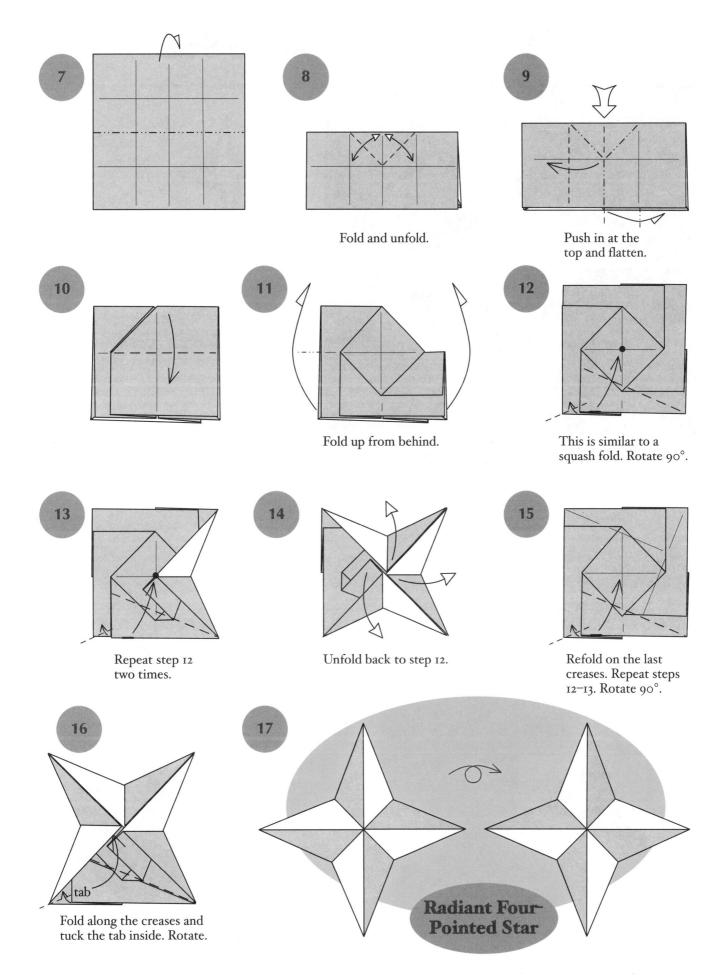

7

8

Fold and unfold.

9

Push in at the top and flatten.

10

11

Fold up from behind.

12

This is similar to a squash fold. Rotate 90°.

13

Repeat step 12 two times.

14

Unfold back to step 12.

15

Refold on the last creases. Repeat steps 12–13. Rotate 90°.

16

Fold along the creases and tuck the tab inside. Rotate.

tab

17

Radiant Four-Pointed Star

Four-Pointed Woven Star

Designed by Russell Cashdollar

This woven star is a rare discovery. Each side is composed of three strips of alternating dark and light matter. This interplay of matter has caused astronomers to reevaluate their very theories of the Universe. Can you explain it?

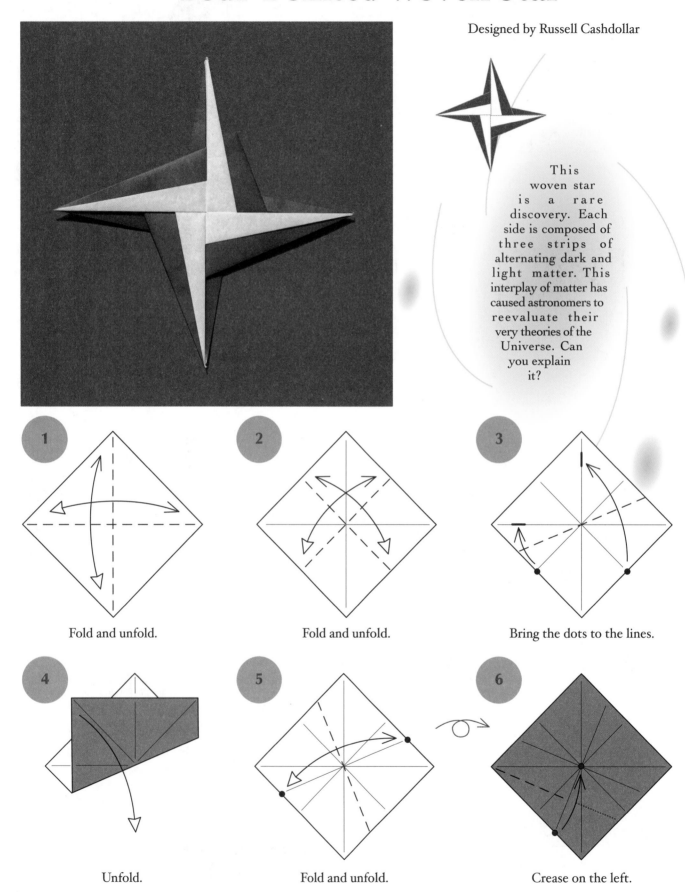

1 Fold and unfold.

2 Fold and unfold.

3 Bring the dots to the lines.

4 Unfold.

5 Fold and unfold.

6 Crease on the left.

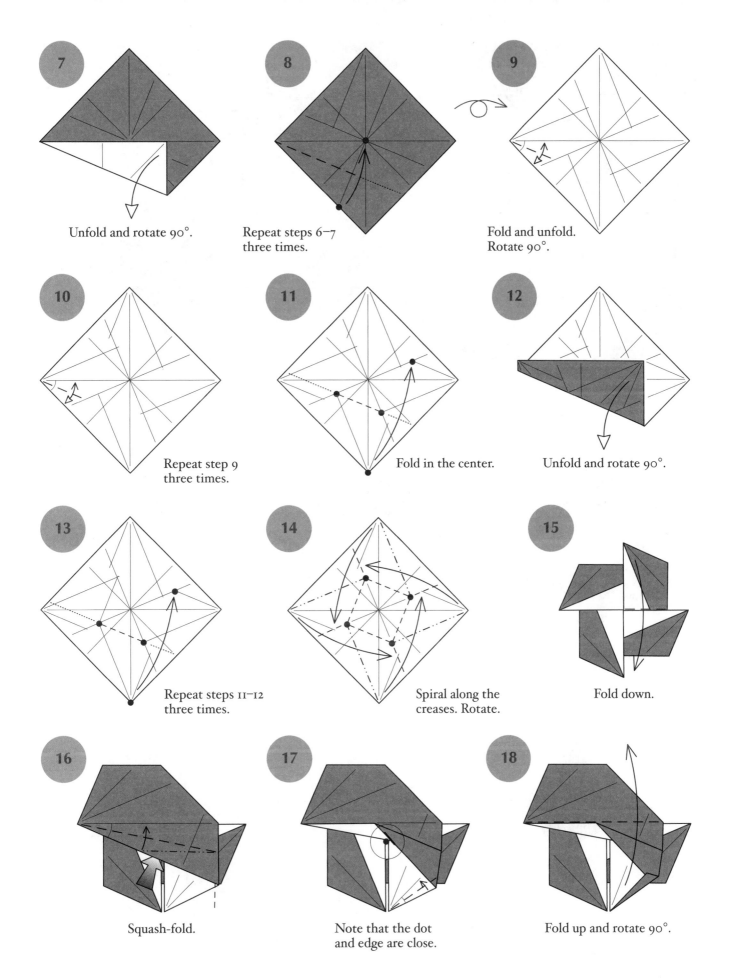

7 Unfold and rotate 90°.

8 Repeat steps 6–7 three times.

9 Fold and unfold. Rotate 90°.

10 Repeat step 9 three times.

11 Fold in the center.

12 Unfold and rotate 90°.

13 Repeat steps 11–12 three times.

14 Spiral along the creases. Rotate.

15 Fold down.

16 Squash-fold.

17 Note that the dot and edge are close.

18 Fold up and rotate 90°.

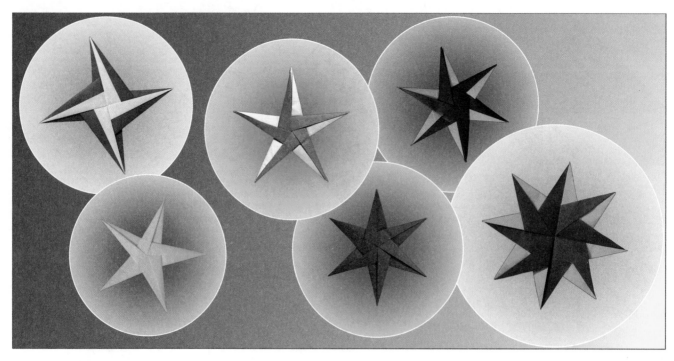

Woven Stars

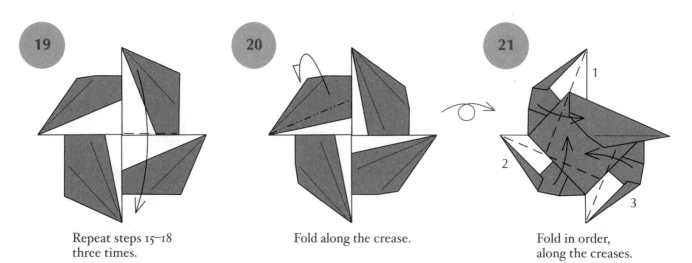

19 Repeat steps 15–18 three times.

20 Fold along the crease.

21 Fold in order, along the creases.

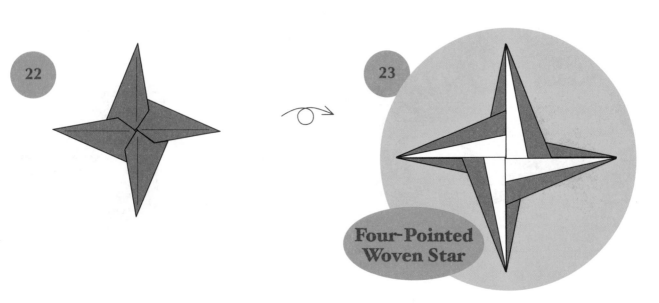

22

23

Four-Pointed Woven Star

Fancy Pinwheels

Designed by Russell Cashdollar

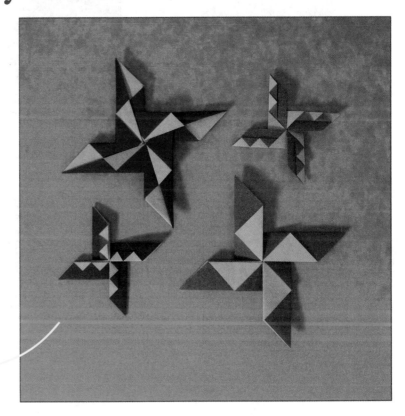

Colorful pinwheels are found in many star clusters. Once one is found, several related ones are often found nearby. Here is a collection of four related pinwheels. After folding these, see if you can design more.

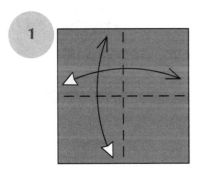

1

Fold and unfold.

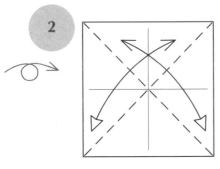

2

Fold and unfold.

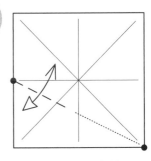

3

Fold and unfold.

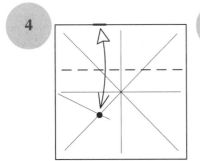

4

Fold and unfold.

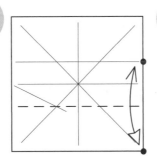

5

Fold and unfold.

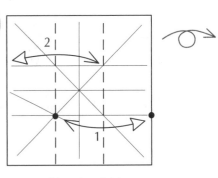

6

Fold and unfold.

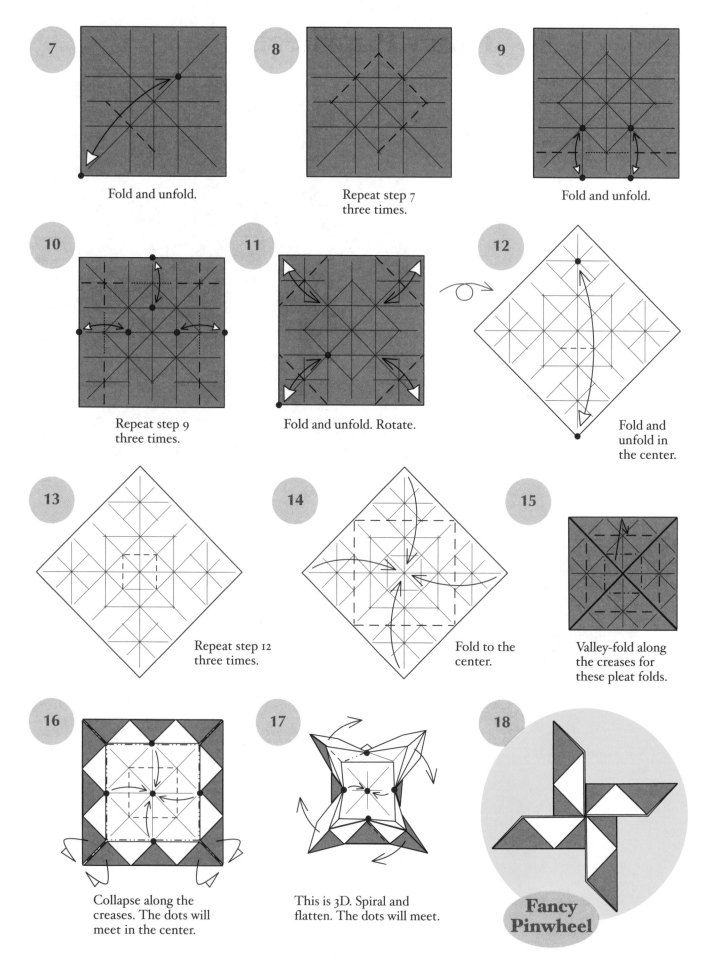

7 Fold and unfold.

8 Repeat step 7 three times.

9 Fold and unfold.

10 Repeat step 9 three times.

11 Fold and unfold. Rotate.

12 Fold and unfold in the center.

13 Repeat step 12 three times.

14 Fold to the center.

15 Valley-fold along the creases for these pleat folds.

16 Collapse along the creases. The dots will meet in the center.

17 This is 3D. Spiral and flatten. The dots will meet.

18 **Fancy Pinwheel**

Fancy Pinwheel Variation A

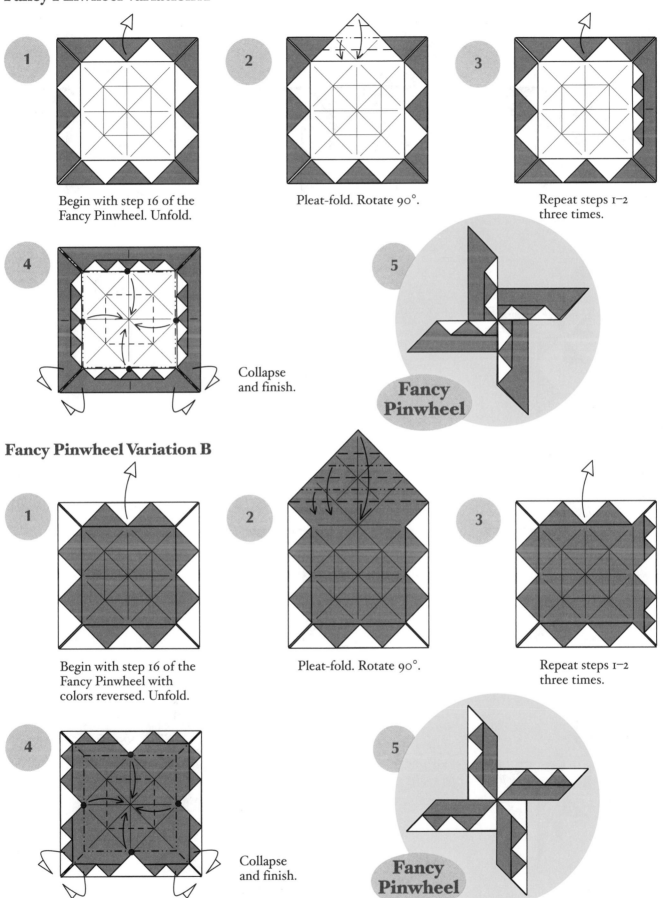

1 Begin with step 16 of the Fancy Pinwheel. Unfold.

2 Pleat-fold. Rotate 90°.

3 Repeat steps 1–2 three times.

4 Collapse and finish.

5 Fancy Pinwheel

Fancy Pinwheel Variation B

1 Begin with step 16 of the Fancy Pinwheel with colors reversed. Unfold.

2 Pleat-fold. Rotate 90°.

3 Repeat steps 1–2 three times.

4 Collapse and finish.

5 Fancy Pinwheel

Kaleidoscopic Pinwheel

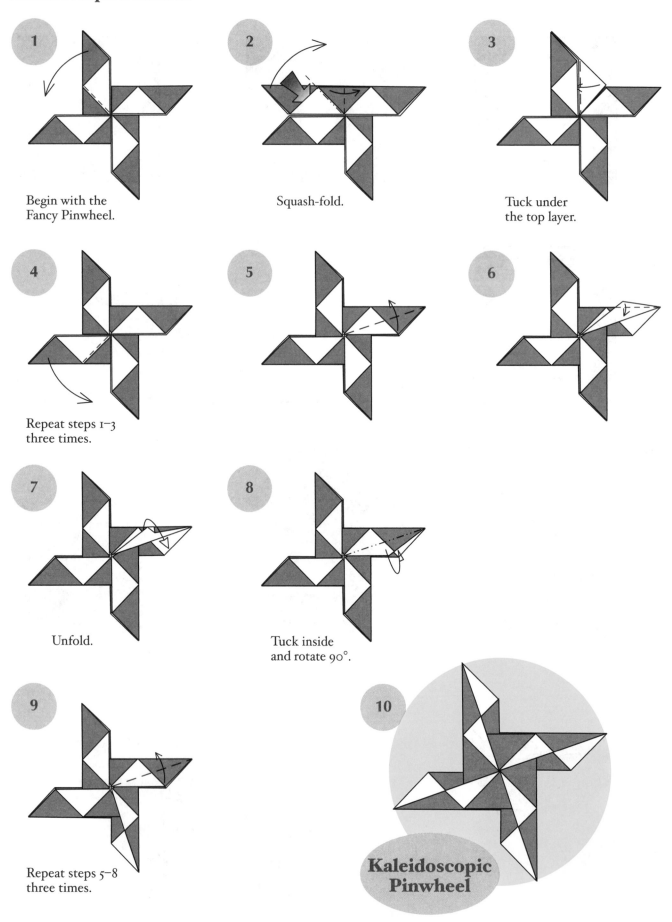

1 Begin with the Fancy Pinwheel.

2 Squash-fold.

3 Tuck under the top layer.

4 Repeat steps 1–3 three times.

5

6

7 Unfold.

8 Tuck inside and rotate 90°.

9 Repeat steps 5–8 three times.

10 Kaleidoscopic Pinwheel

Kaleidoscopic Square

Designed by Russell Cashdollar,
modified by John Montroll

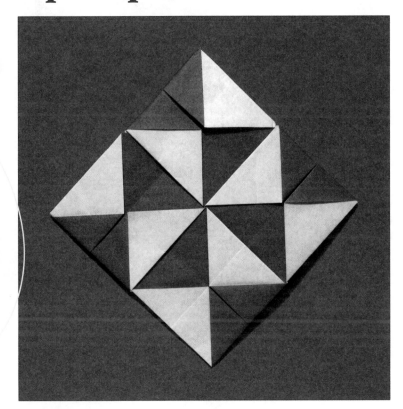

This
Kaleidoscopic Square
has a stunning colorful pattern.
When you visit this star, be prepared
to experience regional extremes of hot
and cold on its surface. Russell
Cashdollar introduced me to this clever
design which I then modified into the version
seen here. Steps 3 to 6 set up the landmark
which simplifies the folding structure;
folding such a wild model in such
a simple way is what origami
is all about.

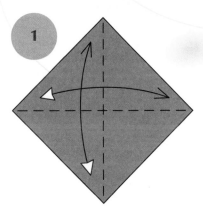

1

Fold and unfold.

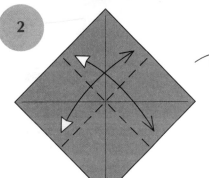

2

Fold and unfold.

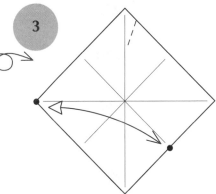

3

Fold and unfold
at the top.

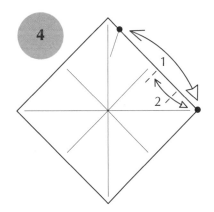

4

Fold and unfold
on the edge.

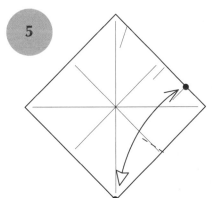

5

Fold and unfold
on the edge.

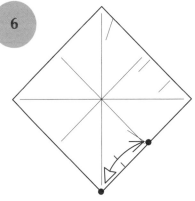

6

Fold and unfold
on the edge.

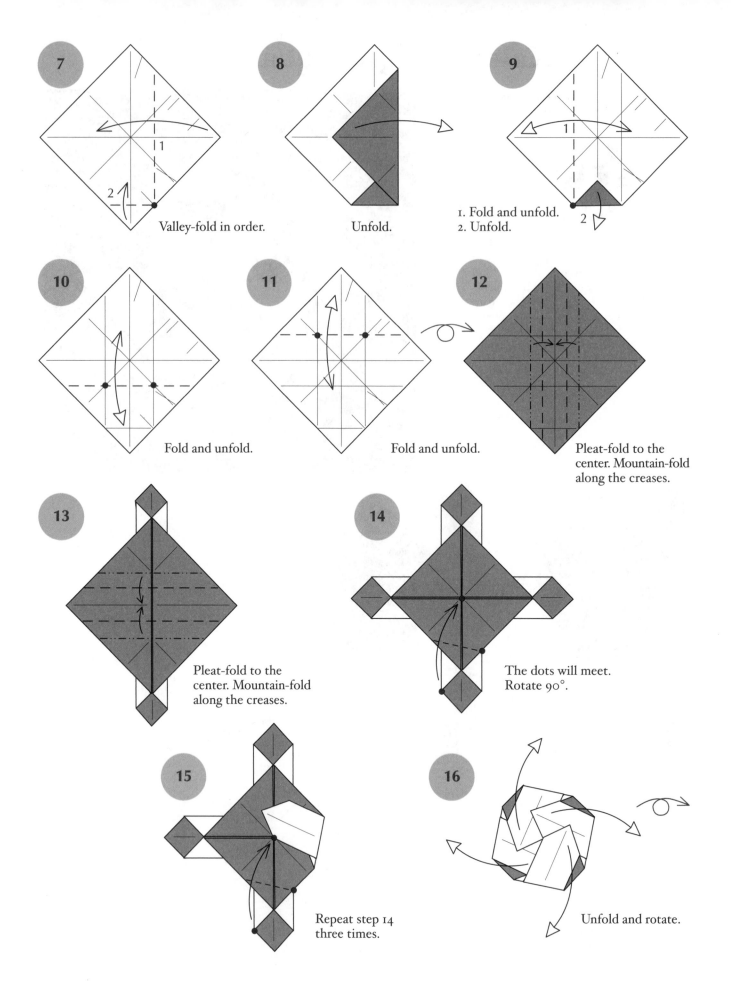

7 Valley-fold in order.

8 Unfold.

9 1. Fold and unfold.
2. Unfold.

10 Fold and unfold.

11 Fold and unfold.

12 Pleat-fold to the center. Mountain-fold along the creases.

13 Pleat-fold to the center. Mountain-fold along the creases.

14 The dots will meet. Rotate 90°.

15 Repeat step 14 three times.

16 Unfold and rotate.

Kaleidoscopic Stars

17

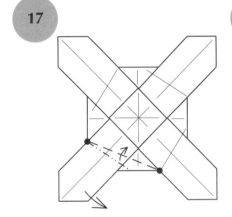

Pleat-fold. Mountain-fold along the crease. Rotate 90°.

18

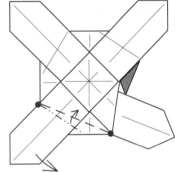

Repeat step 17 three times.

19

The dots will meet. Rotate 90°.

20

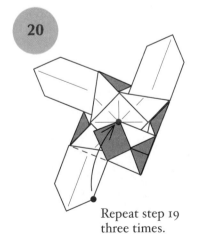

Repeat step 19 three times.

21

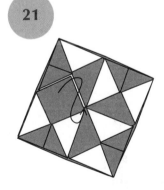

Tuck inside. Rotate.

22

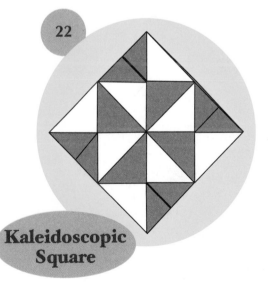

Kaleidoscopic Square

Intersecting Squares

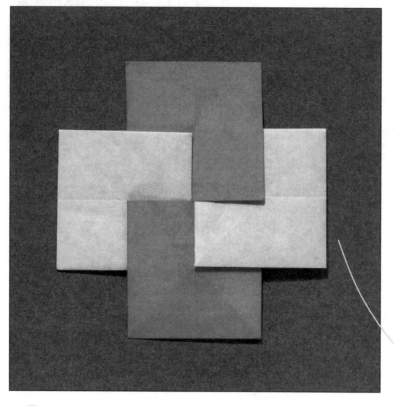

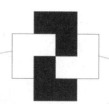

When first discovered, this object appeared to be a star with most unusual properties. With recent advances and further investigation, it was found to actually consist of colliding galaxies. Be careful when approaching this massive conglomeration. Once you have captured this cosmic display along with the others in this section, you will become Master of the four-pointed stars.

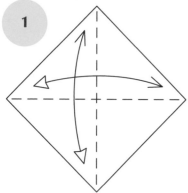

1

Fold and unfold.

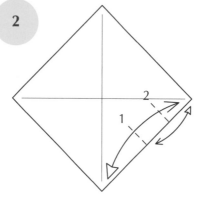

2

Fold and unfold on the edge to find the quarter mark.

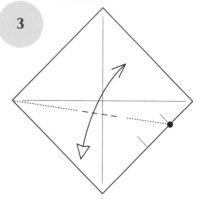

3

Fold and unfold by the diagonal.

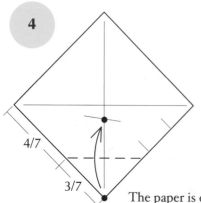

4

4/7

3/7

The paper is divided into sevenths.

5

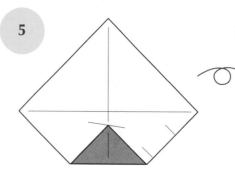

6

Fold to the center and swing out from behind.

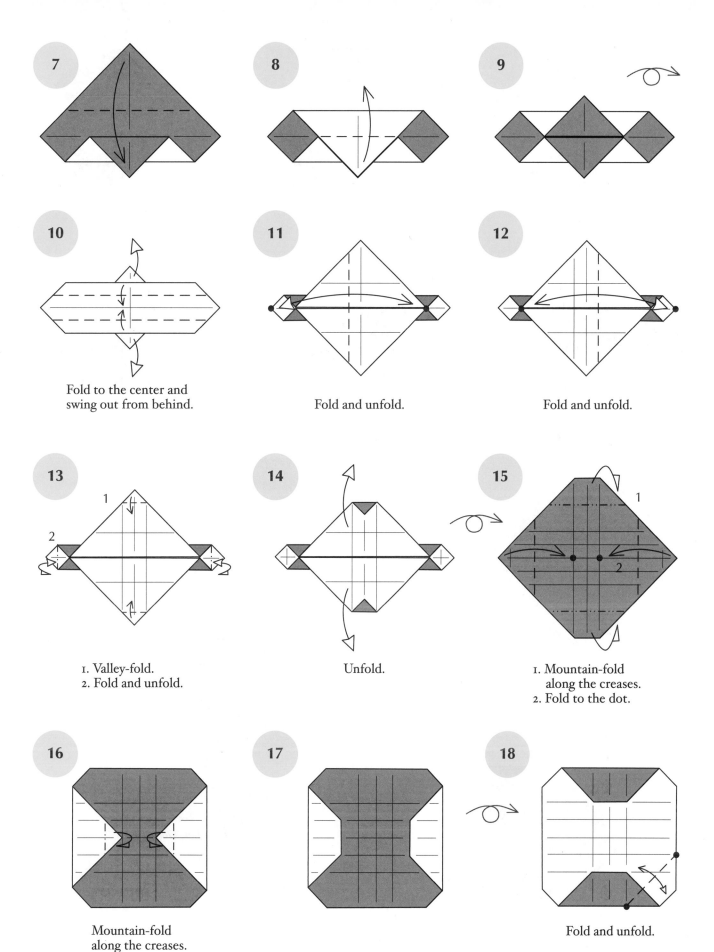

7

8

9

10

Fold to the center and
swing out from behind.

11

Fold and unfold.

12

Fold and unfold.

13

1. Valley-fold.
2. Fold and unfold.

14

Unfold.

15

1. Mountain-fold
   along the creases.
2. Fold to the dot.

16

Mountain-fold
along the creases.

17

18

Fold and unfold.

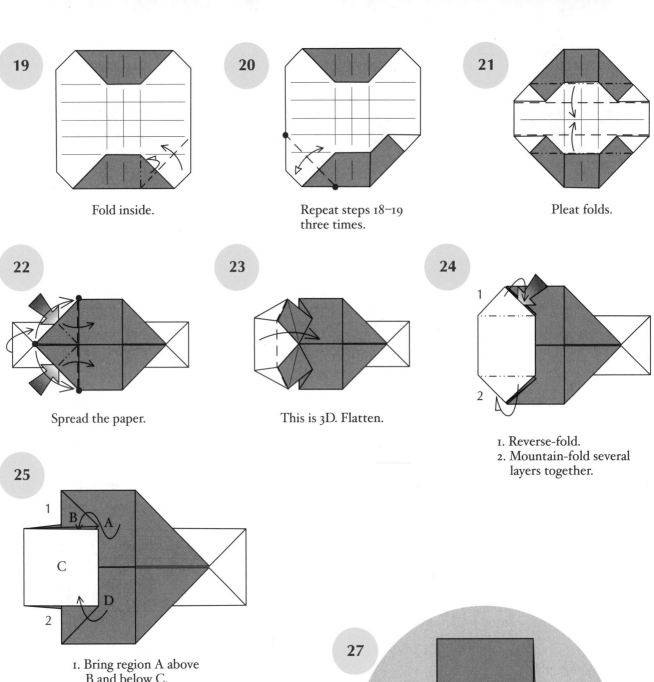

19

Fold inside.

20

Repeat steps 18–19 three times.

21

Pleat folds.

22

Spread the paper.

23

This is 3D. Flatten.

24

1. Reverse-fold.
2. Mountain-fold several layers together.

25

1. Bring region A above B and below C.
2. Bring D above C. Rotate 180°.

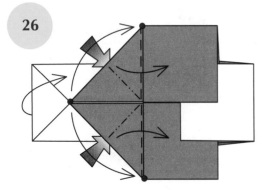

26

Repeat steps 22–25.

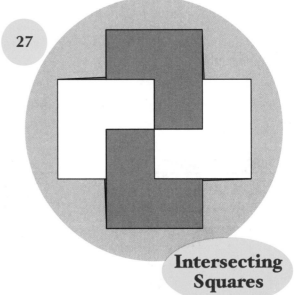

27

Intersecting Squares

Stars with Five Points

Five-pointed stars fill every arm in every galaxy. The secret to these beautiful stars is in their pentagonal embryonic formation. Most in this collection begin with a pentagon formed from a square. Some are solid colored, some multicolored, and some are woven.

Five-Pointed Star

This is the one five-pointed star which is not based upon a pentagon. On step 6, a rectangle is formed with a diagonal of 36°. This is the angle at the vertex of each of the five points, and tabs lock the model.

This famous shape is perfect to fold and present as a prize or award.

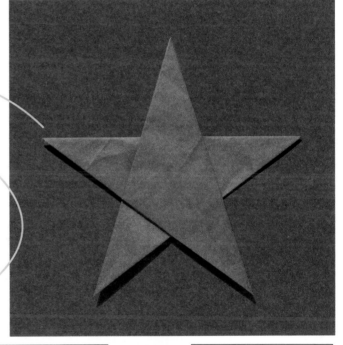

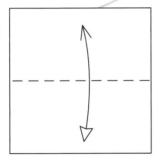

1

Fold and unfold.

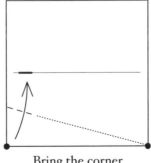

2

Bring the corner to the line.

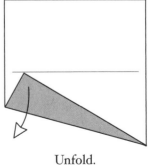

3

Unfold.

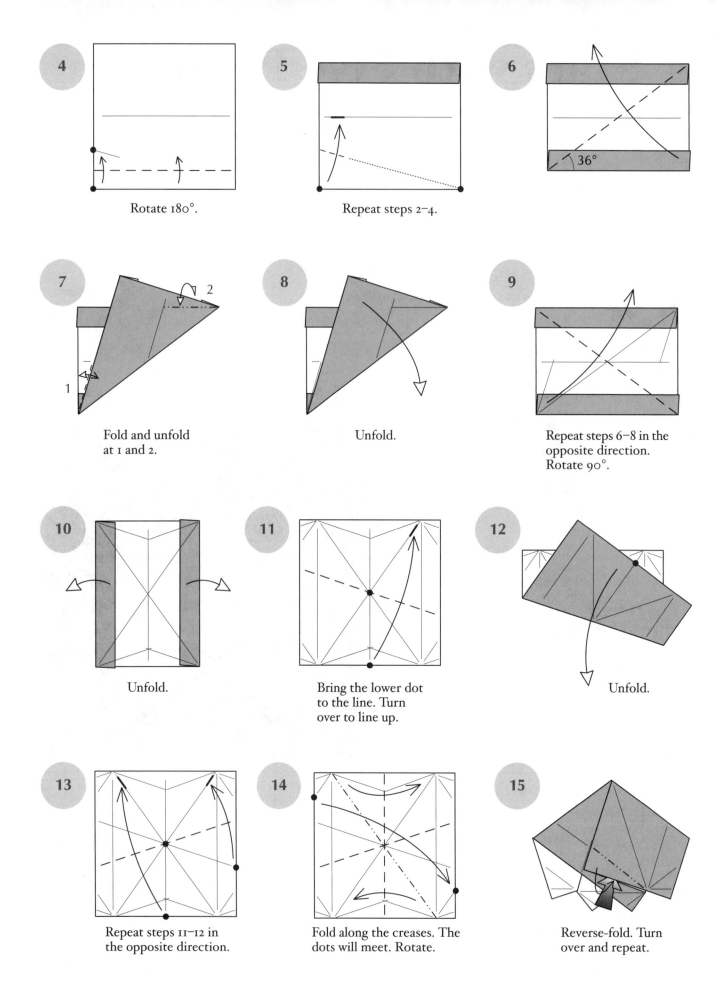

4 Rotate 180°.

5 Repeat steps 2–4.

6 36°

7 Fold and unfold at 1 and 2.

8 Unfold.

9 Repeat steps 6–8 in the opposite direction. Rotate 90°.

10 Unfold.

11 Bring the lower dot to the line. Turn over to line up.

12 Unfold.

13 Repeat steps 11–12 in the opposite direction.

14 Fold along the creases. The dots will meet. Rotate.

15 Reverse-fold. Turn over and repeat.

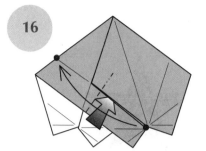

16

Reverse-fold. Turn
over and repeat.

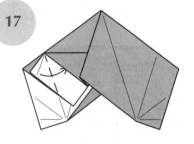

17

Fold along the crease
to tuck inside. Turn
over and repeat.

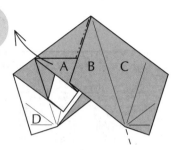

18

Slide the paper. Turn over and
repeat. Follow A, B, C, and D
into the next step. Rotate.

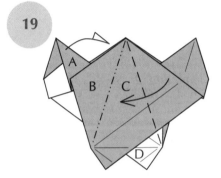

19

Fold all the layers.

20

Tuck inside. Turn
over and repeat.

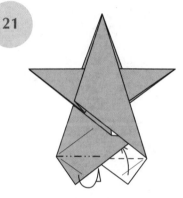

21

Tuck inside. Turn
over and repeat.

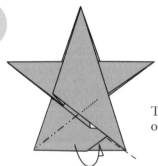

22

Tuck inside. Turn
over and repeat.

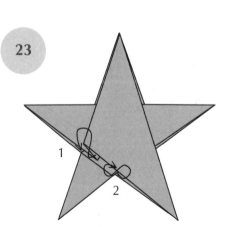

23

1. Tuck the tab into the pocket.
   Turn over and repeat.
2. Tuck the hidden tab into the
   hidden tab just above.

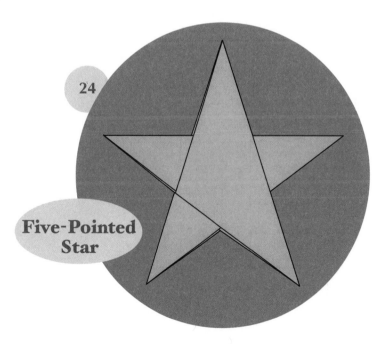

24

**Five-Pointed
Star**

Five-Pointed Star

This star is from a pentagon. I developed a method to fold the square into a pentagon (see step 13) with as few steps as possible so that all the angles at the corners are exact.

1

Fold and unfold
on the edge.

2

Fold and unfold,
creasing lightly.

3

Fold and unfold
at the bottom to
bisect the angle.

4

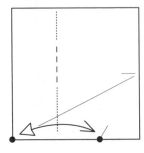

Fold and unfold
in the center.

5

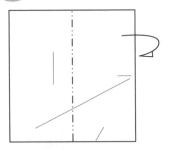

Fold in half.

6

36°

Bring the corner to the
crease. Repeat behind.
The 36° angle is exact.

7

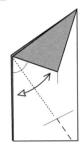

Fold and unfold the
top layer at the bottom
to bisect the angle.

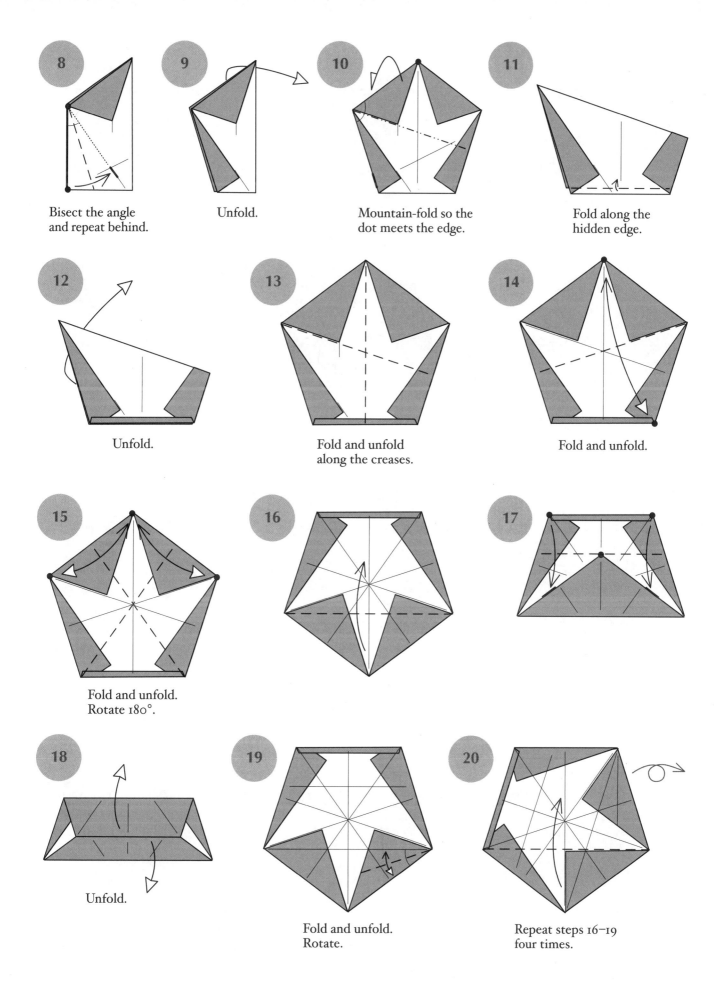

8 Bisect the angle and repeat behind.

9 Unfold.

10 Mountain-fold so the dot meets the edge.

11 Fold along the hidden edge.

12 Unfold.

13 Fold and unfold along the creases.

14 Fold and unfold.

15 Fold and unfold. Rotate 180°.

16

17

18 Unfold.

19 Fold and unfold. Rotate.

20 Repeat steps 16–19 four times.

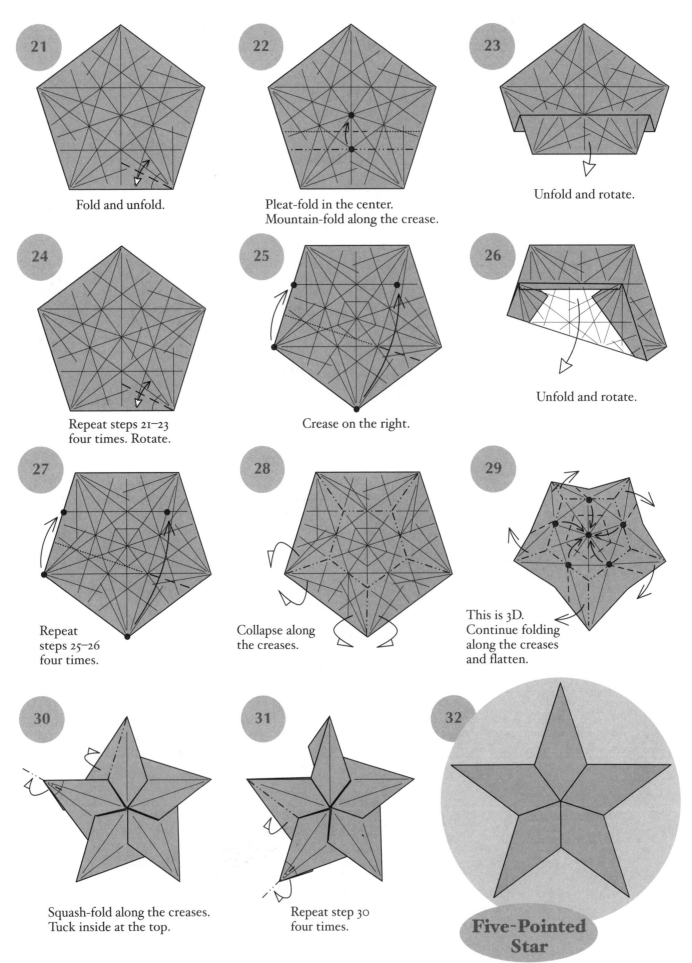

21 Fold and unfold.

22 Pleat-fold in the center. Mountain-fold along the crease.

23 Unfold and rotate.

24 Repeat steps 21–23 four times. Rotate.

25 Crease on the right.

26 Unfold and rotate.

27 Repeat steps 25–26 four times.

28 Collapse along the creases.

29 This is 3D. Continue folding along the creases and flatten.

30 Squash-fold along the creases. Tuck inside at the top.

31 Repeat step 30 four times.

32 Five-Pointed Star

Radiant Five-Pointed Star

This radiant star has a stunning color pattern. The folding method is similar to the previous 5-pointed star. For a life-size version, begin with a sheet of origami paper where each side is 902,508 miles long.

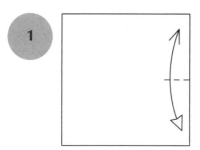

1 Fold and unfold on the edge.

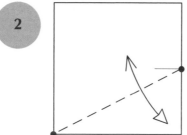

2 Fold and unfold, creasing lightly.

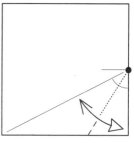

3 Fold and unfold at the bottom to bisect the angle.

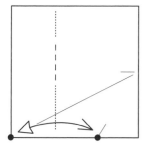

4 Fold and unfold in the center.

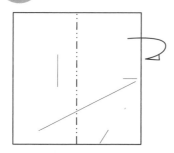

5 Fold in half.

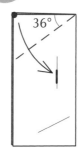

6 Bring the corner to the crease. Repeat behind. The 36° angle is exact.

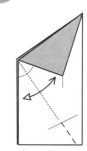

7 Fold and unfold the top layer at the bottom to bisect the angle.

Radiant Five-Pointed Star 47

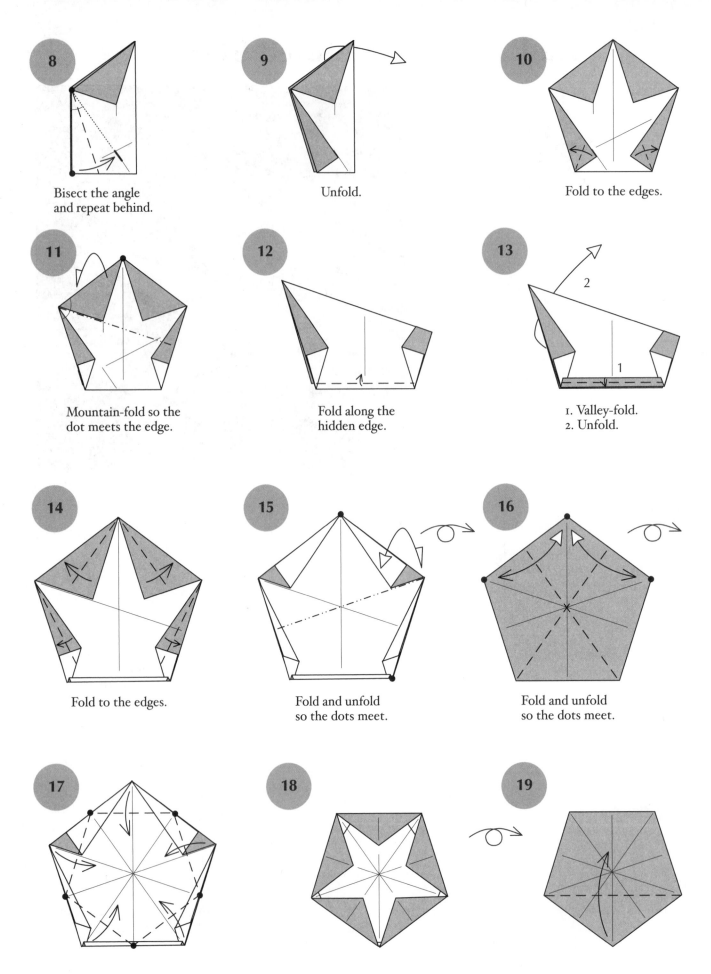

8 Bisect the angle and repeat behind.

9 Unfold.

10 Fold to the edges.

11 Mountain-fold so the dot meets the edge.

12 Fold along the hidden edge.

13
1. Valley-fold.
2. Unfold.

14 Fold to the edges.

15 Fold and unfold so the dots meet.

16 Fold and unfold so the dots meet.

17

18

19

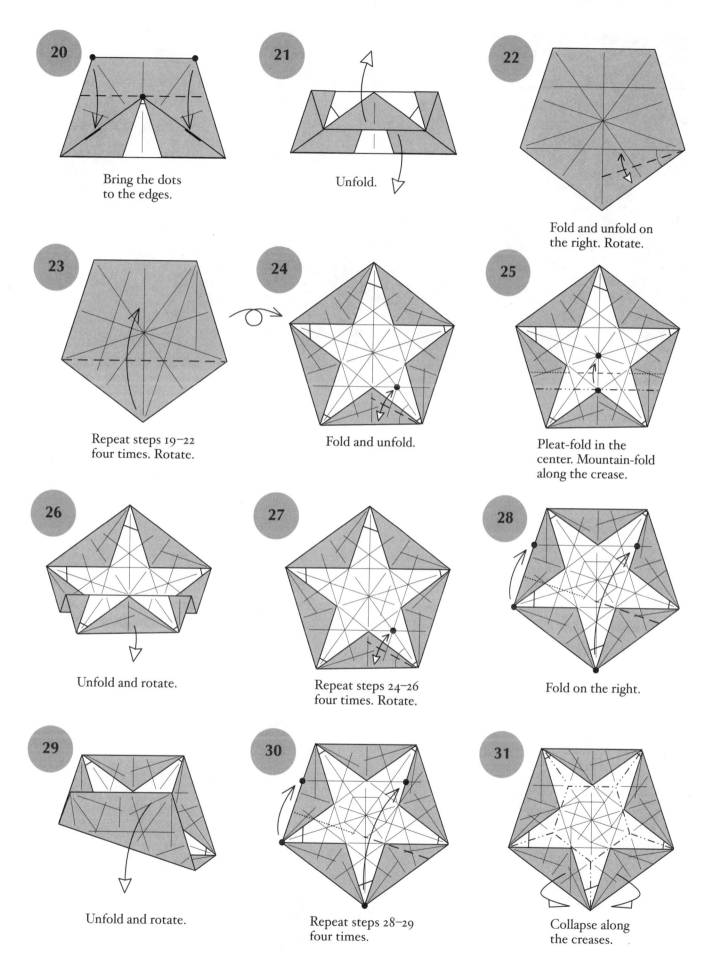

20 Bring the dots to the edges.

21 Unfold.

22 Fold and unfold on the right. Rotate.

23 Repeat steps 19–22 four times. Rotate.

24 Fold and unfold.

25 Pleat-fold in the center. Mountain-fold along the crease.

26 Unfold and rotate.

27 Repeat steps 24–26 four times. Rotate.

28 Fold on the right.

29 Unfold and rotate.

30 Repeat steps 28–29 four times.

31 Collapse along the creases.

Star Mobile

32 This is 3D. Continue folding along the creases and flatten.

33 Squash-fold along the creases. Tuck inside at the top.

34 Repeat step 33 four times.

35 **Radiant Five-Pointed Star**

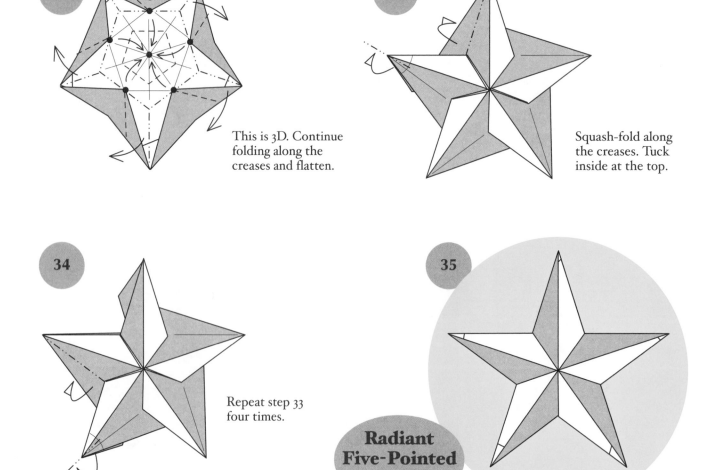

Woven Five-Pointed Star

Woven stars display beautiful effects. This special star was formed in a cosmic blink of 1,000 years but your goal is to capture it in under an hour. If you can do so, you will be awarded this star.

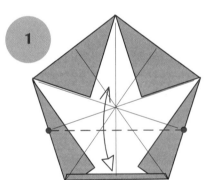

1

Begin with step 16 of the Five-Pointed Star on page 44. Fold and unfold. Rotate.

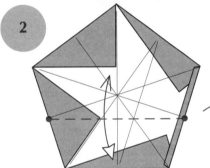

2

Repeat step 1 four times.

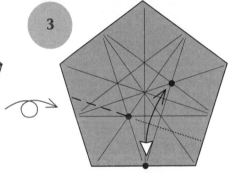

3

Fold and unfold. Crease on the left. Rotate.

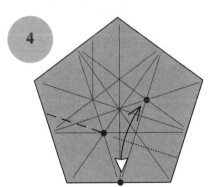

4

Repeat step 3 four times.

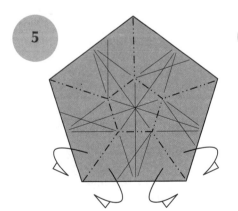

5

Collapse along the creases.

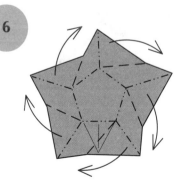

6

This is 3D. Continue folding along the creases and flatten.

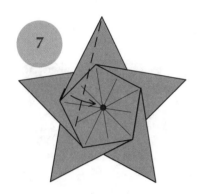

7

Bring the edge
to the center.

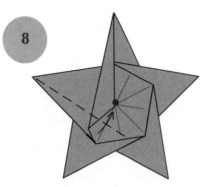

8

Repeat step 7 four times.

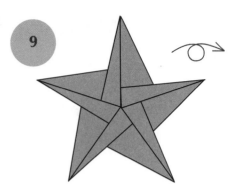

9

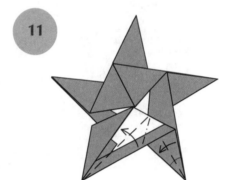

10

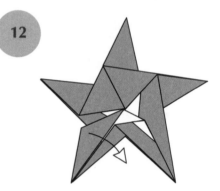

11

Squash-fold.

12

Unfold.

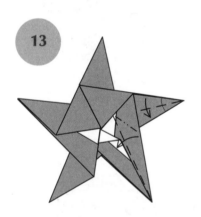

13

Repeat steps 11–12
four more times.

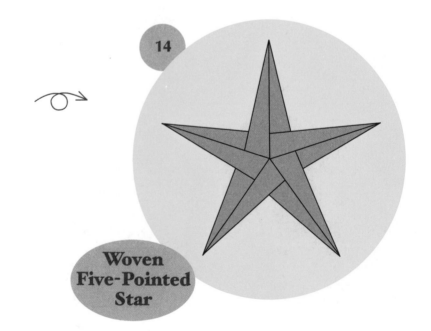

14

**Woven
Five-Pointed
Star**

Colorful Woven Five-Pointed Star

The folding method for this star is similar to the previous woven star. Due to its woven properties, this star can also be displayed with the woven six-pointed stars in the next section. Once you have captured it, along with the other five-pointed stars, you will become Master of the five-pointed stars on your quest to becoming Master of the Universe.

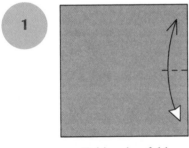

1 Fold and unfold on the edge.

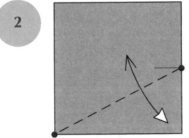

2 Fold and unfold, creasing lightly.

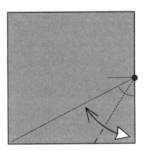

3 Fold and unfold at the bottom to bisect the angle.

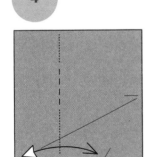

4 Fold and unfold in the center.

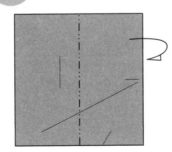

5 Fold in half.

6 Bring the corner to the crease. Repeat behind. The 36° angle is exact.

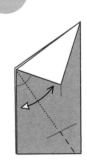

7 Fold and unfold the top layer at the bottom to bisect the angle.

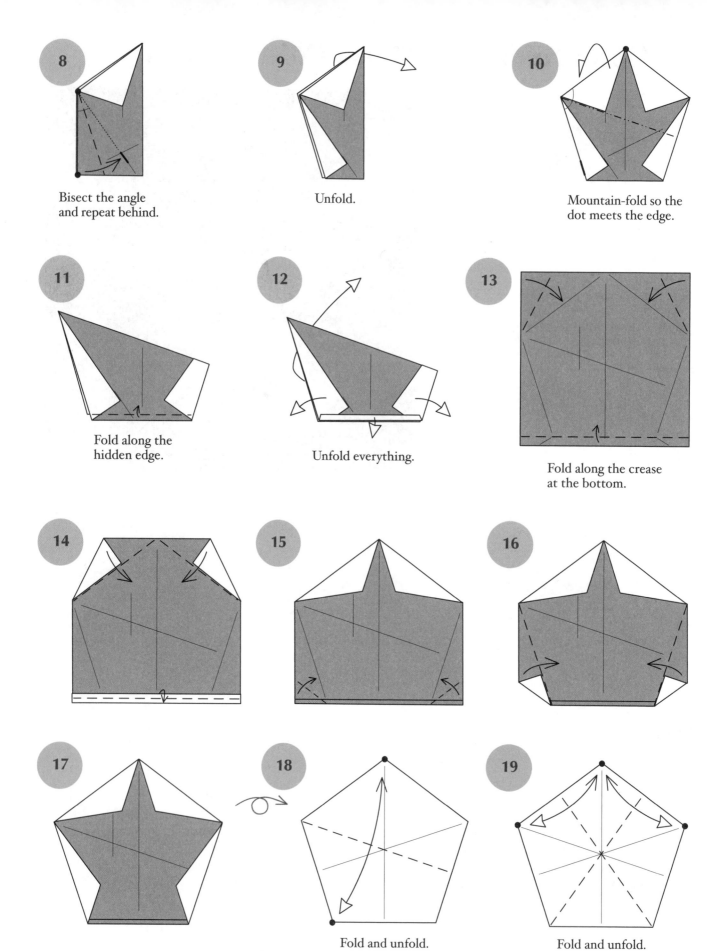

8 Bisect the angle and repeat behind.

9 Unfold.

10 Mountain-fold so the dot meets the edge.

11 Fold along the hidden edge.

12 Unfold everything.

13 Fold along the crease at the bottom.

14

15

16

17

18 Fold and unfold.

19 Fold and unfold.

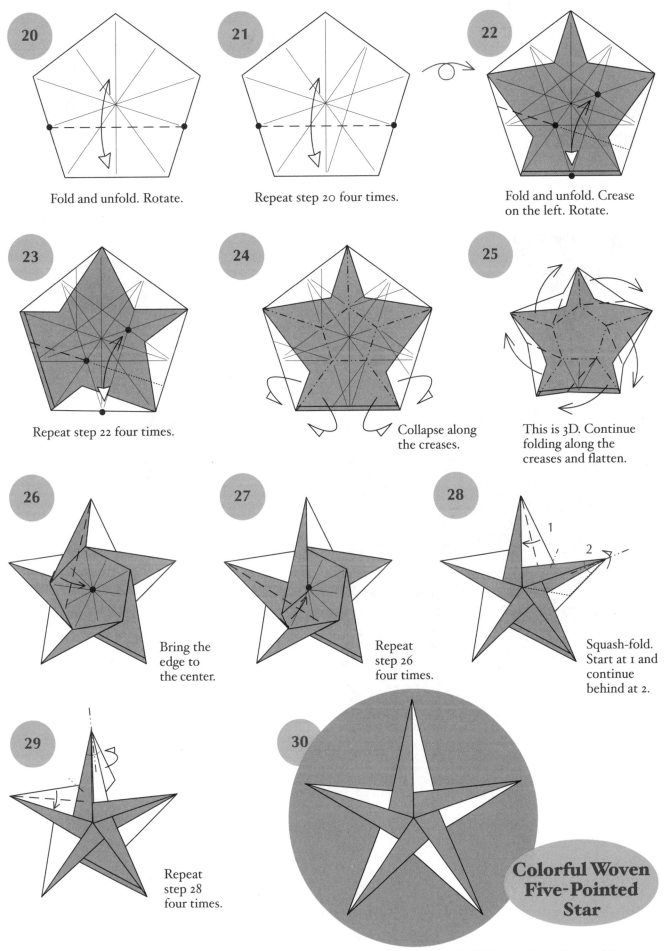

20 Fold and unfold. Rotate.

21 Repeat step 20 four times.

22 Fold and unfold. Crease on the left. Rotate.

23 Repeat step 22 four times.

24 Collapse along the creases.

25 This is 3D. Continue folding along the creases and flatten.

26 Bring the edge to the center.

27 Repeat step 26 four times.

28 Squash-fold. Start at 1 and continue behind at 2.

29 Repeat step 28 four times.

30

Colorful Woven Five-Pointed Star

Colorful Woven Five-Pointed Star 55

Stars with Six Points

A s the universe expanded, stars with six points began appearing everywhere. Now, a wide variety can be found, from the simple and plain to the majestically wild Kaleidoscopic and Radioactive Stars. Radiant and woven varieties have also been discovered. These stars are based upon hexagonal structures. For the multicolored stars, unusually patterned hexagons are used, to realize the finished effect.

Six-Pointed Star

W e begin this section with a relatively simple star. Some of the more elaborate stars use similar techniques. The square is folded into the largest possible hexagon which is collapsed into this star. Many stars are formed from collapsed polygons.

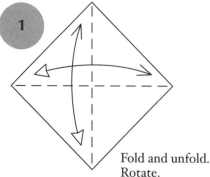

1 Fold and unfold. Rotate.

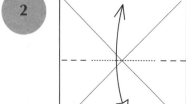

2 Fold and unfold on the edges.

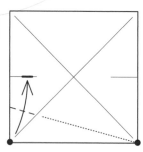

3 Bring the corner to the crease.

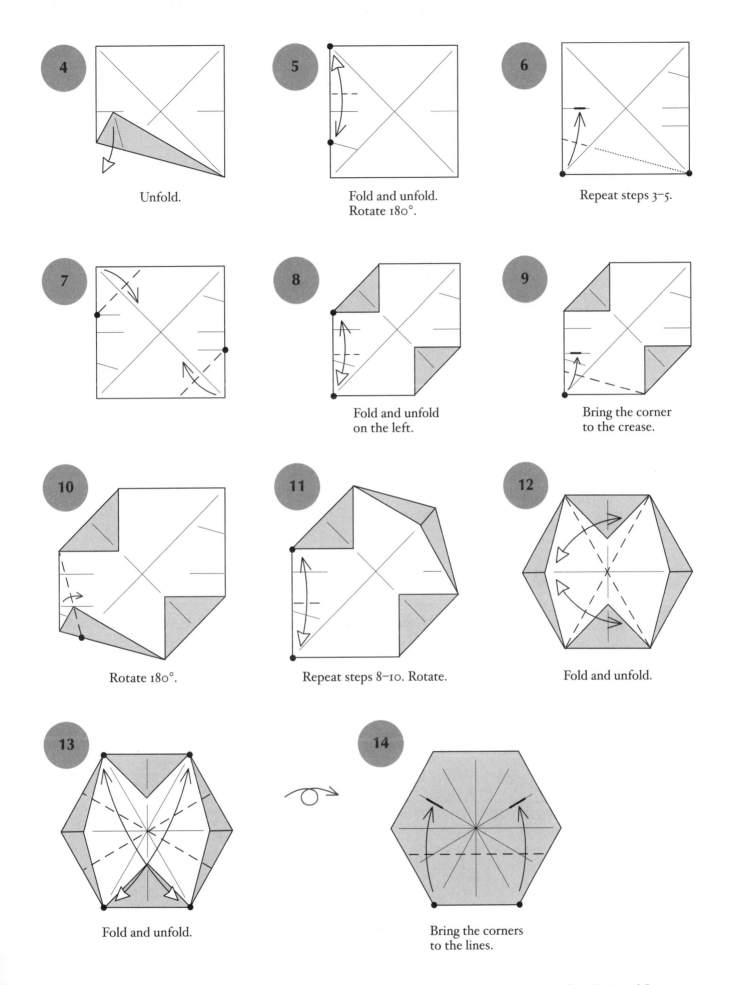

4   Unfold.

5   Fold and unfold.
Rotate 180°.

6   Repeat steps 3–5.

7

8   Fold and unfold
on the left.

9   Bring the corner
to the crease.

10   Rotate 180°.

11   Repeat steps 8–10. Rotate.

12   Fold and unfold.

13   Fold and unfold.

14   Bring the corners
to the lines.

Six-Pointed Star   57

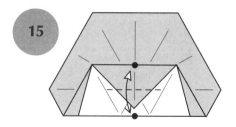

15 Fold and unfold in the center.

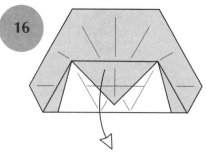

16 Unfold and rotate.

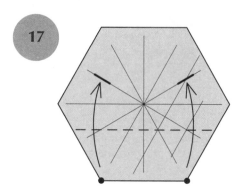

17 Repeat steps 14–16 five times.

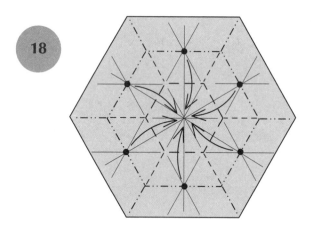

18 Collapse along the creases. The dots will go to the center as the model becomes 3D.

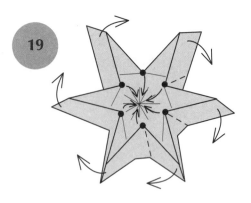

19 The dots will meet in the center. Flatten.

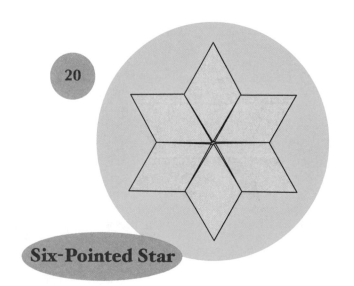

20 Six-Pointed Star

Radiant Six-Pointed Star

Radiant stars are fun to capture and fold. Other radiant stars found here are the three, four, and five-pointed stars. The folding method is similar to the previous star, and takes the same number of steps. The hexagon used, to allow the alternating color pattern, is shown in step 16.

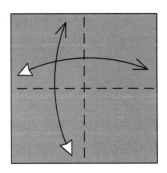

Fold and unfold.

Bring the dot to the line.
Crease on the bottom.

Unfold.

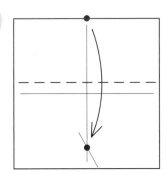

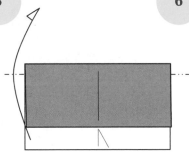

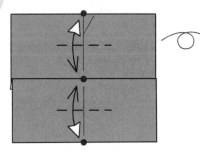

Fold along the crease.

Fold and unfold
in the center.

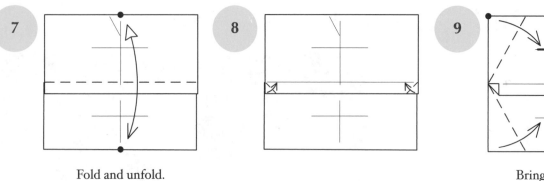
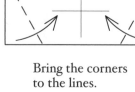

7 Fold and unfold.

8

9 Bring the corners to the lines.

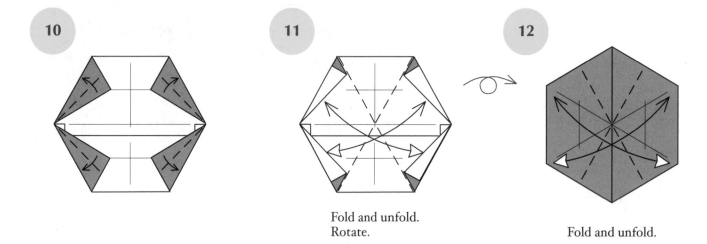

10

11 Fold and unfold. Rotate.

12 Fold and unfold.

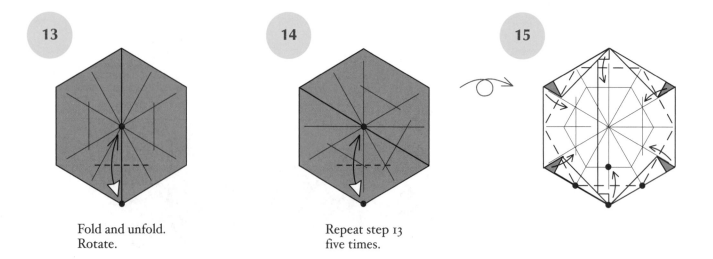

13 Fold and unfold. Rotate.

14 Repeat step 13 five times.

15

16

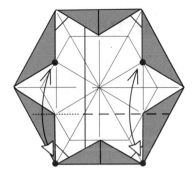

Fold and unfold.
Rotate.

17

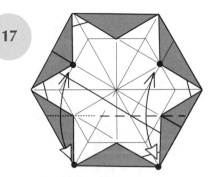

Repeat step 16
five times.

18

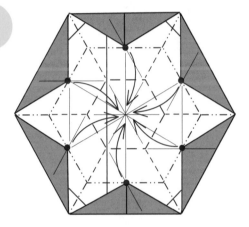

Collapse along the creases.
The dots will go to the center
as the model becomes 3D.

19

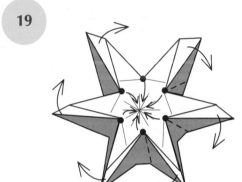

The dots will meet in
the center. Flatten.

20

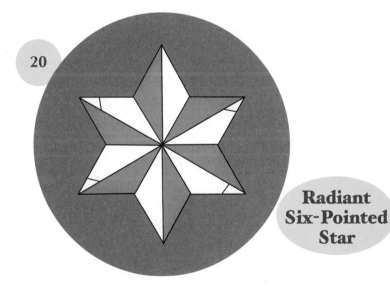

**Radiant
Six-Pointed
Star**

Six-Sided Propeller

This propeller can be found spinning rapidly among the stars. To capture it, you must slow it down by using a magnetic decelerator. The folding procedure ends with spiral folding.

1

Fold and unfold.
Rotate.

2

Fold and unfold
on the edges.

3

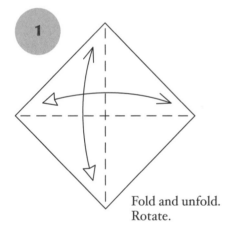

Bring the corner
to the crease.

4

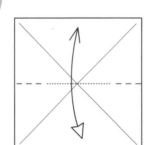

Unfold.

5

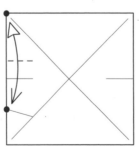

Fold and unfold.
Rotate 180°.

6

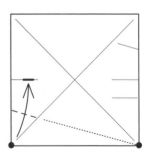

Repeat steps 3–5.

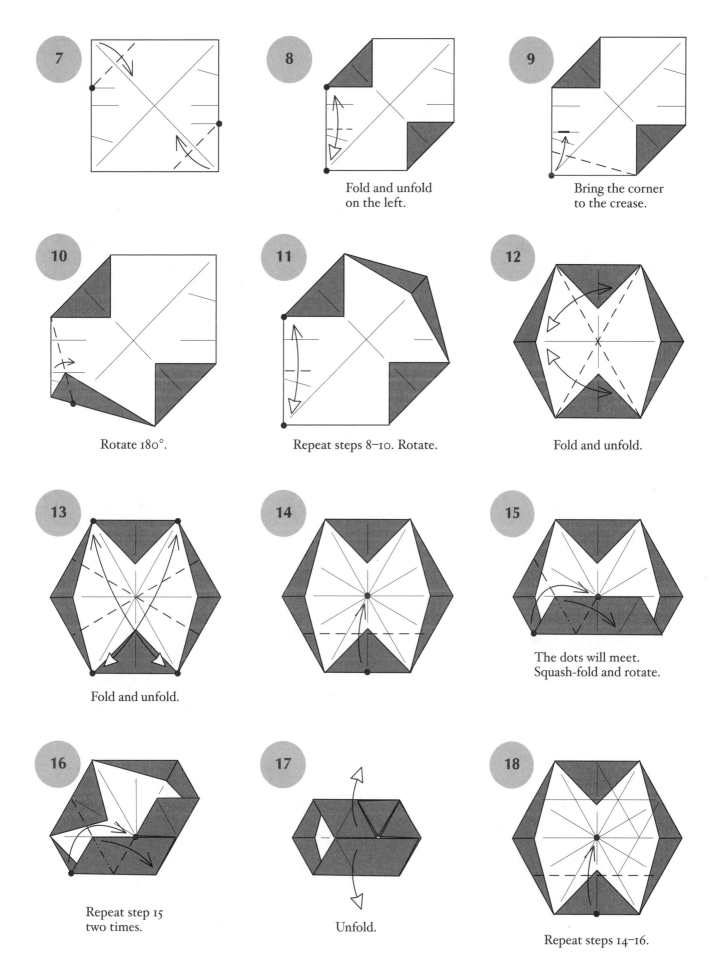

7

8

Fold and unfold
on the left.

9

Bring the corner
to the crease.

10

Rotate 180°.

11

Repeat steps 8–10. Rotate.

12

Fold and unfold.

13

Fold and unfold.

14

15

The dots will meet.
Squash-fold and rotate.

16

Repeat step 15
two times.

17

Unfold.

18

Repeat steps 14–16.

Propellers

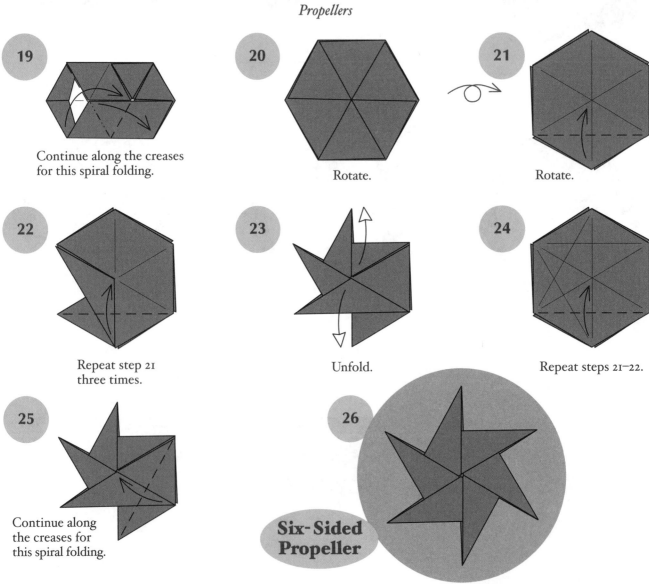

19 Continue along the creases for this spiral folding.

20 Rotate.

21 Rotate.

22 Repeat step 21 three times.

23 Unfold.

24 Repeat steps 21–22.

25 Continue along the creases for this spiral folding.

26 **Six-Sided Propeller**

Colorful Propeller

The Colorful Propeller uses a folding method which is similar to the previous Propeller. The patterned hexagon is shown in step 21, but only the back side is drawn. The other side (if you turn over that figure) will reveal the color pattern. The first few steps of the folding process are seemingly random folds, making you wonder how these could lead to anything.

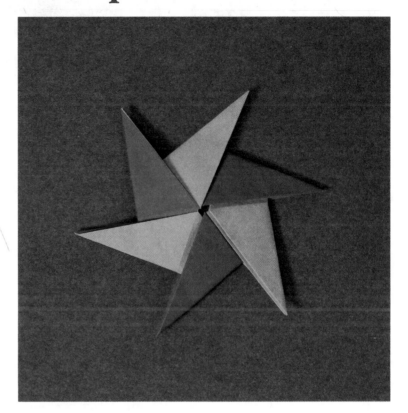

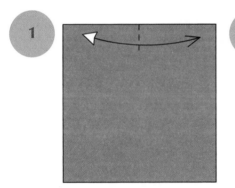

Fold and unfold on the top.

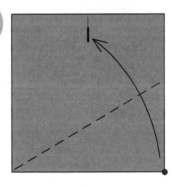

Bring the corner to the line.

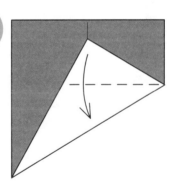

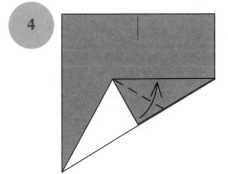

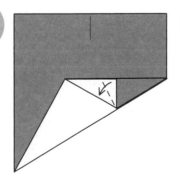

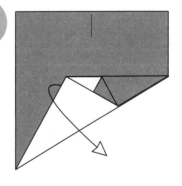

Unfold.

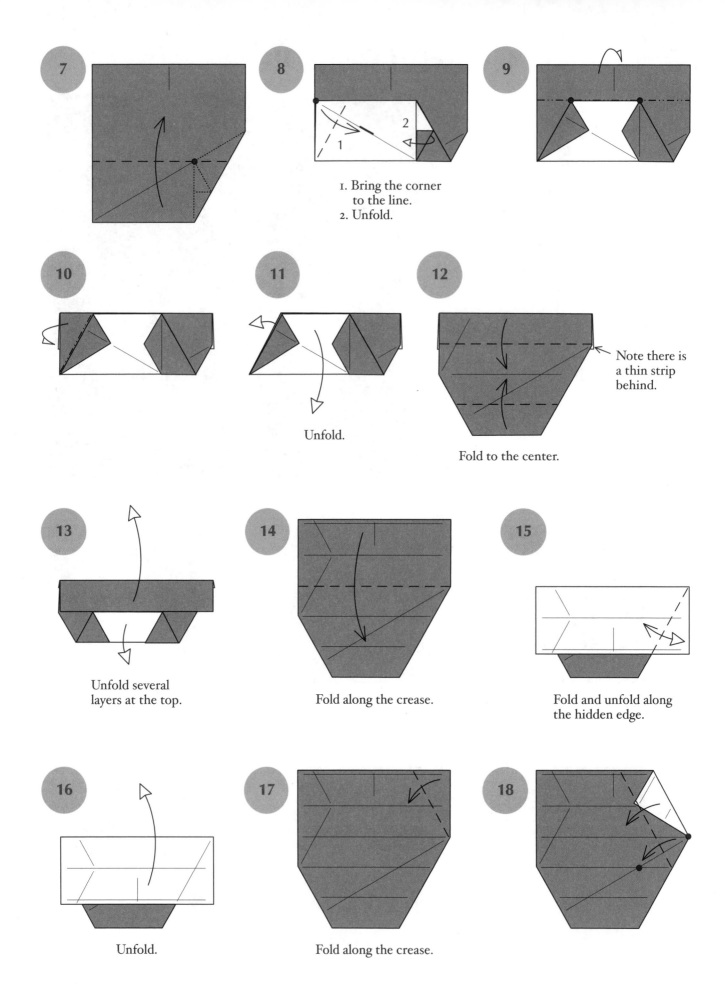

7

8

1. Bring the corner
to the line.
2. Unfold.

9

10

11

Unfold.

12

Note there is
a thin strip
behind.

Fold to the center.

13

Unfold several
layers at the top.

14

Fold along the crease.

15

Fold and unfold along
the hidden edge.

16

Unfold.

17

Fold along the crease.

18

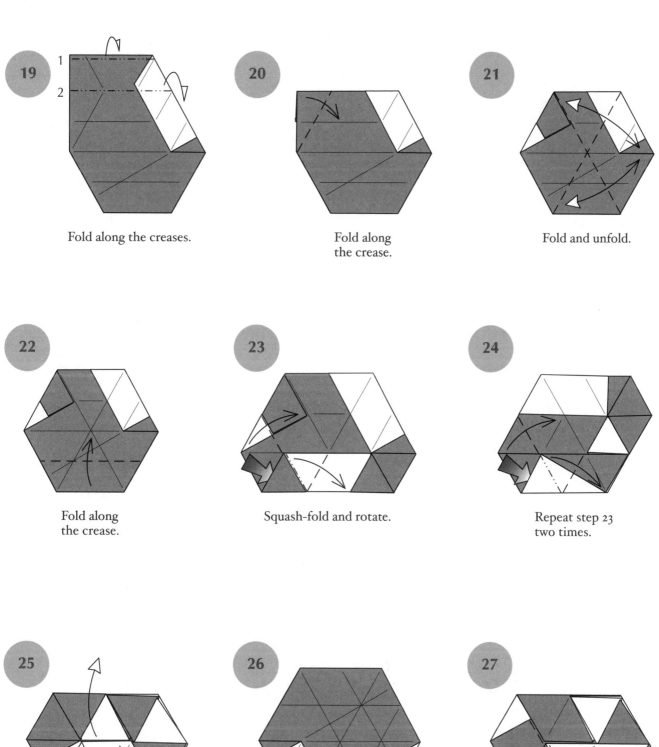

19 Fold along the creases.

20 Fold along the crease.

21 Fold and unfold.

22 Fold along the crease.

23 Squash-fold and rotate.

24 Repeat step 23 two times.

25 Unfold.

26 Repeat steps 22–24.

27 Continue along the creases for this spiral folding.

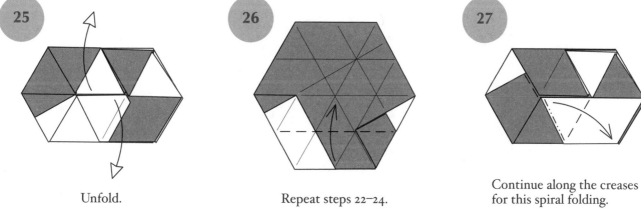

Colorful Propeller 67

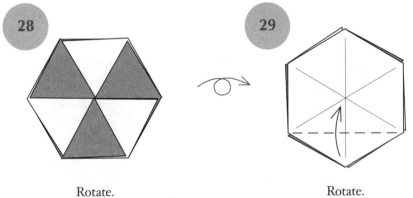

28 Rotate.

29 Rotate.

30 Repeat step 29 three times.

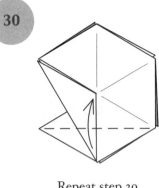

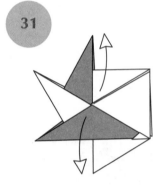

31 Unfold.

32 Repeat steps 29–30.

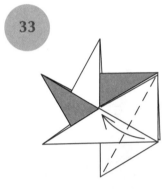

33 Continue along the creases for this spiral folding.

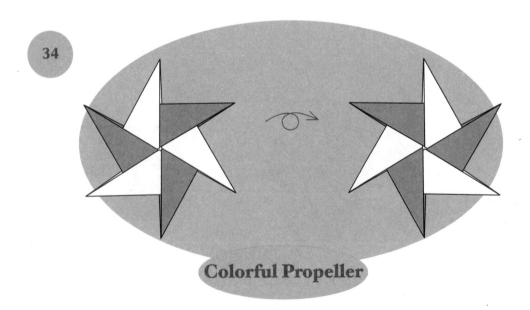

34

Colorful Propeller

Woven Six-Pointed Star

Woven stars yield pleasing effects. Yet it would be dangerous to visit such stars due to their windy environment and gamma rays. The technique used for this woven star is similar to the Woven Five-Pointed star, yet would become bulky if applied to a heptagon for a Woven Seven-Pointed Star.

1

Fold and unfold.
Rotate.

2

Fold and unfold
on the edges.

3

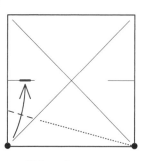

Bring the corner
to the crease.

4

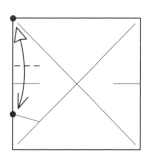

Unfold.

5

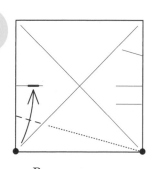

Fold and unfold.
Rotate 180°.

6

Repeat steps 3–5.

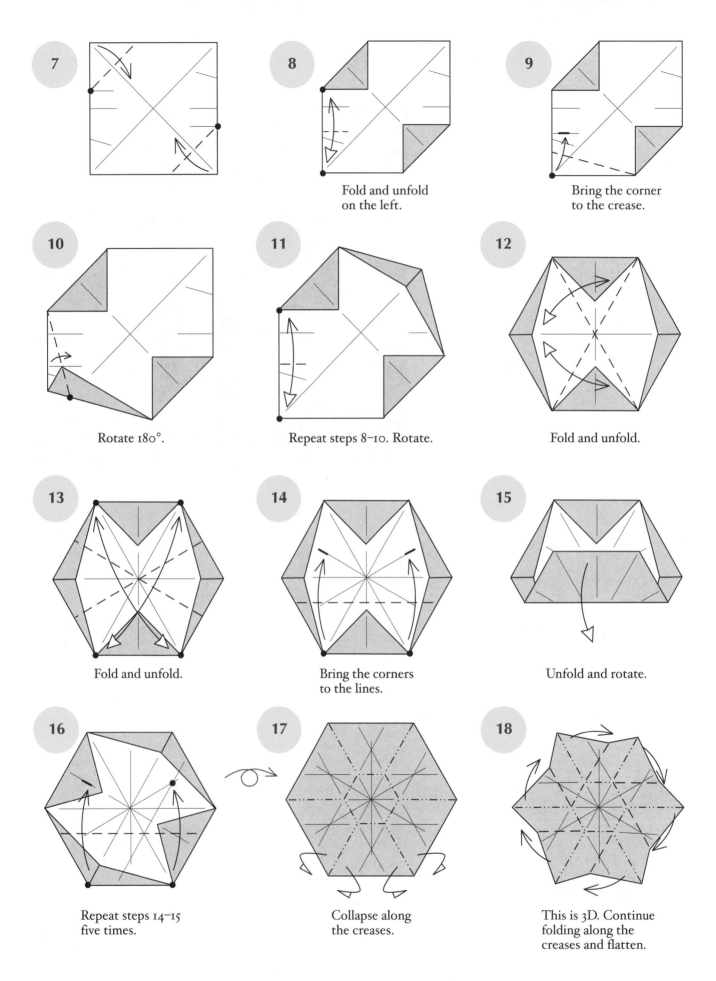

7

8

Fold and unfold
on the left.

9

Bring the corner
to the crease.

10

Rotate 180°.

11

Repeat steps 8–10. Rotate.

12

Fold and unfold.

13

Fold and unfold.

14

Bring the corners
to the lines.

15

Unfold and rotate.

16

Repeat steps 14–15
five times.

17

Collapse along
the creases.

18

This is 3D. Continue
folding along the
creases and flatten.

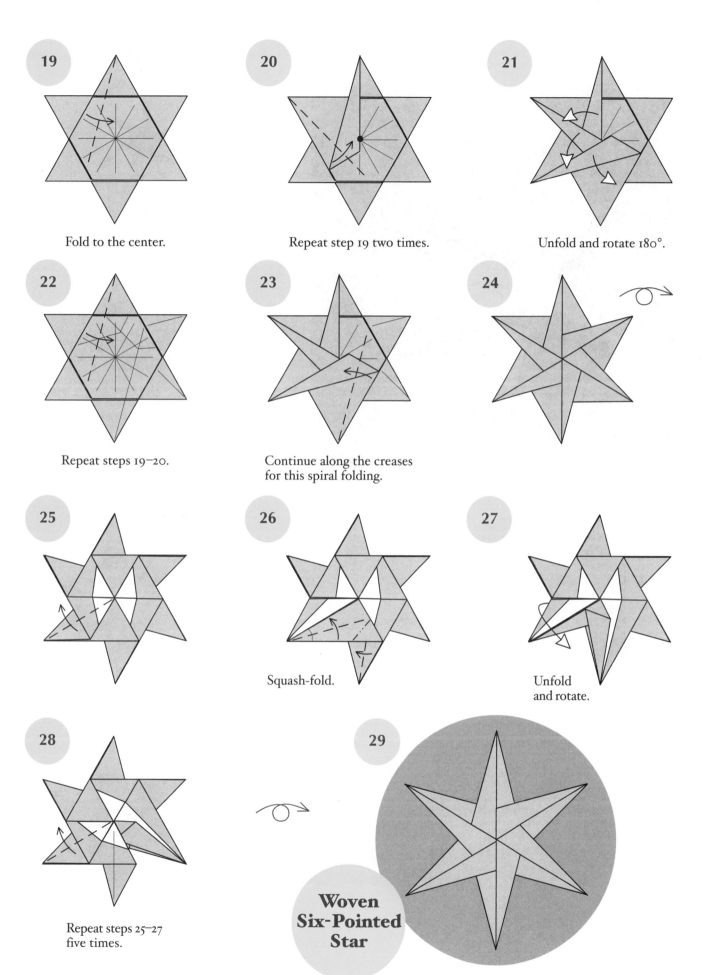

19

Fold to the center.

20

Repeat step 19 two times.

21

Unfold and rotate 180°.

22

Repeat steps 19–20.

23

Continue along the creases for this spiral folding.

24

25

26

Squash-fold.

27

Unfold and rotate.

28

Repeat steps 25–27 five times.

29

Woven Six-Pointed Star

Colorful Woven Six-Pointed Star

This intricately woven star spins in the clockwise direction. It originated from a massive unstable star. Due to gravitational interference, the massive star split in half and the two parts flew into different quadrants of the galaxy. The star shown here is the L-version. The R-Colorful Woven Star spins in the opposite direction. To fold it, simply follow the mirror-image of the diagrams (from step 22 onwards).

1 Fold and unfold.

2 Bring the dot to the line.
Crease on the bottom.

3 Unfold.

4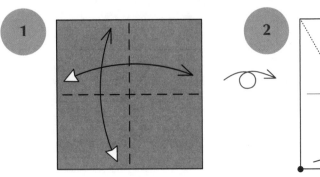

5 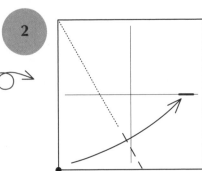 Fold along the crease.

6 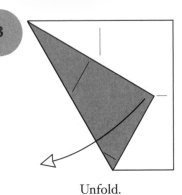 Fold and unfold in the center.

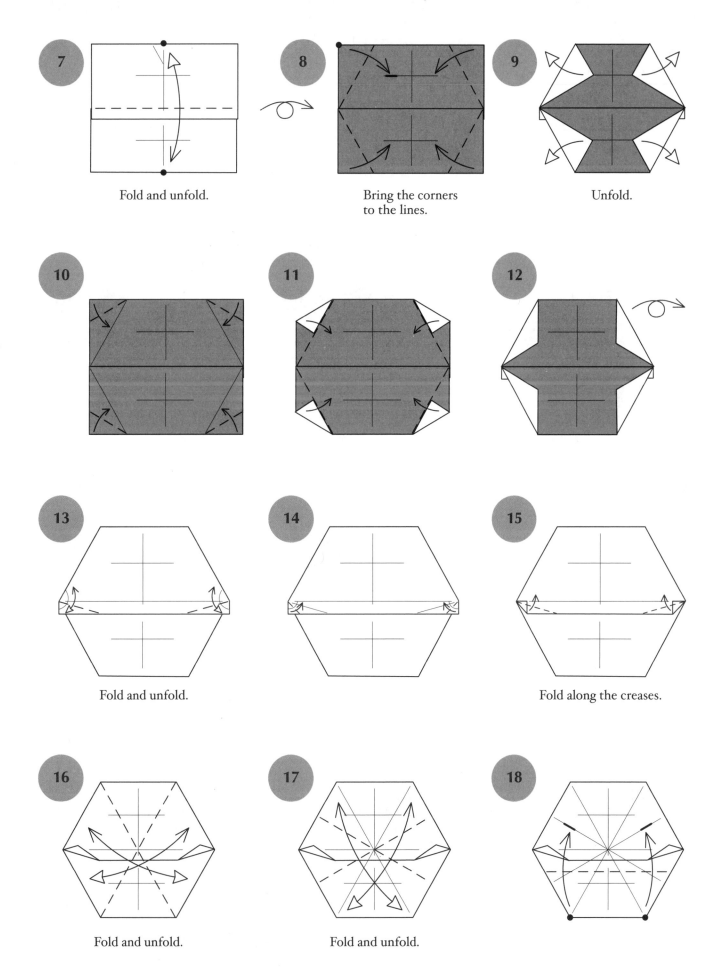

7 Fold and unfold.

8 Bring the corners to the lines.

9 Unfold.

10

11

12

13 Fold and unfold.

14

15 Fold along the creases.

16 Fold and unfold.

17 Fold and unfold.

18

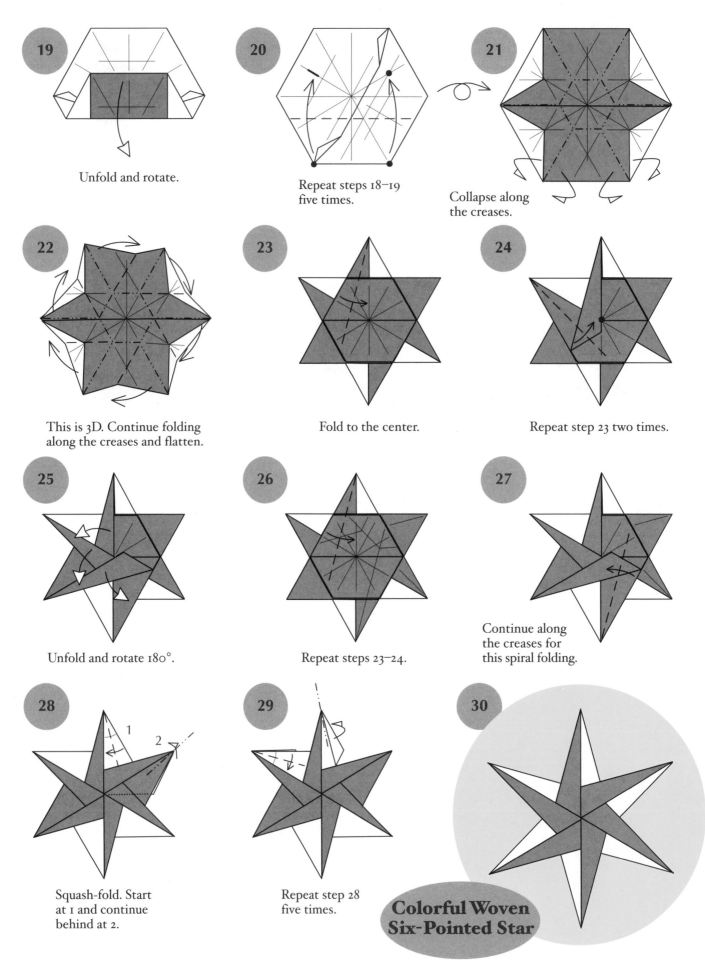

19 Unfold and rotate.

20 Repeat steps 18–19 five times.

21 Collapse along the creases.

22 This is 3D. Continue folding along the creases and flatten.

23 Fold to the center.

24 Repeat step 23 two times.

25 Unfold and rotate 180°.

26 Repeat steps 23–24.

27 Continue along the creases for this spiral folding.

28 Squash-fold. Start at 1 and continue behind at 2.

29 Repeat step 28 five times.

30 Colorful Woven Six-Pointed Star

Fancy Star

The
Fancy Star has
an inner white star.
The hexagon used to
achieve this result is shown
in step 16, where a smaller
white hexagon is embedded
in the larger one. If you
receive this star on your
birthday, you will be
given the gift of
illumination.

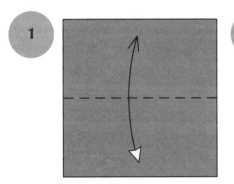

1 Fold and unfold.

2 Fold and unfold.

3 Fold in half.

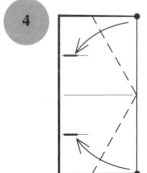

4 Bring the corners to the lines.

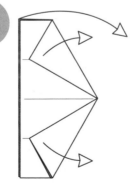

5 Unfold.

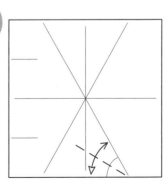

6 Fold and unfold.

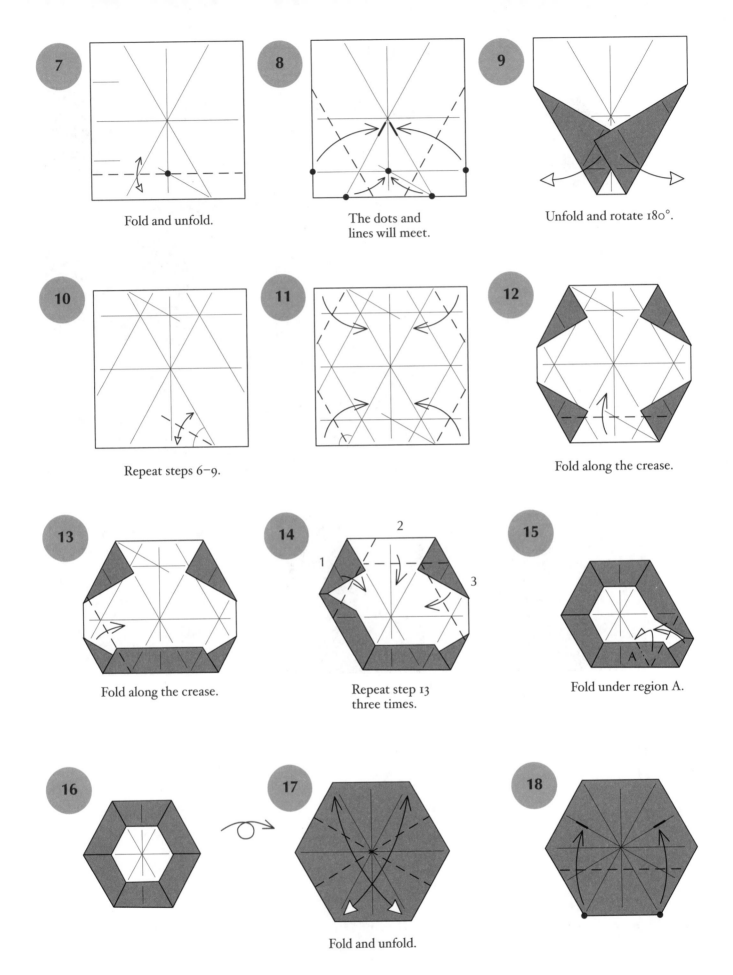

7 Fold and unfold.

8 The dots and lines will meet.

9 Unfold and rotate 180°.

10 Repeat steps 6–9.

11

12 Fold along the crease.

13 Fold along the crease.

14 Repeat step 13 three times.

15 Fold under region A.

16

17 Fold and unfold.

18

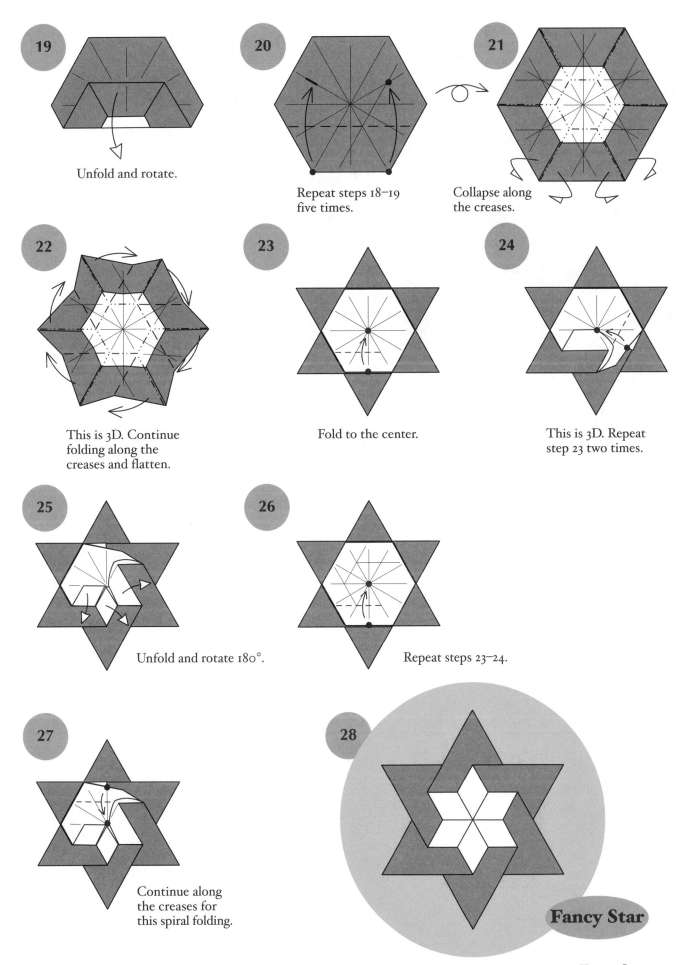

19

Unfold and rotate.

20

Repeat steps 18–19 five times.

21

Collapse along the creases.

22

This is 3D. Continue folding along the creases and flatten.

23

Fold to the center.

24

This is 3D. Repeat step 23 two times.

25

Unfold and rotate 180°.

26

Repeat steps 23–24.

27

Continue along the creases for this spiral folding.

28

Fancy Star

Intersecting Triangles

Color-change models present beautiful and mysterious effects. Two triangular stars of equal mass but different composition once collided and caused the formation of this stable unit. Chemical bonding now makes it impossible to separate this star. Step 24 shows the hexagon with the color pattern which becomes this star when collapsed.

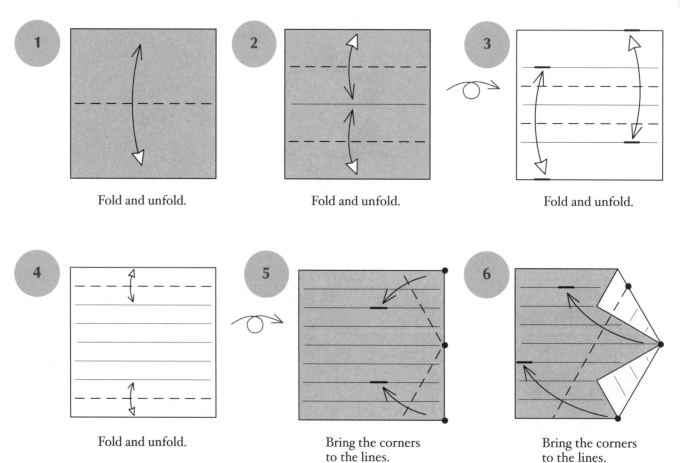

1 Fold and unfold.

2 Fold and unfold.

3 Fold and unfold.

4 Fold and unfold.

5 Bring the corners to the lines.

6 Bring the corners to the lines.

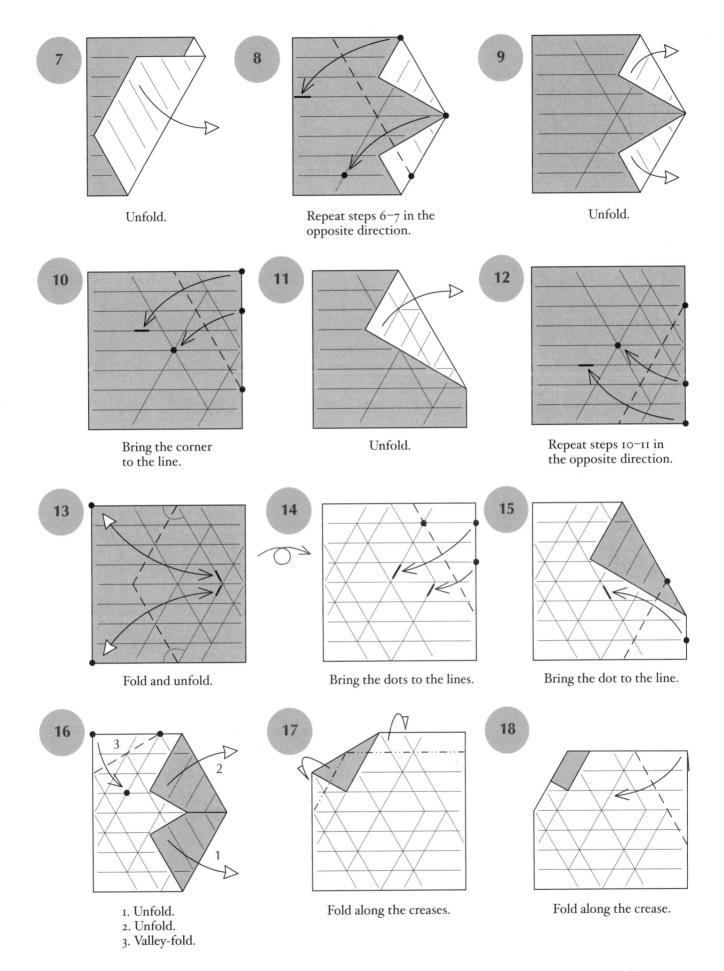

7

Unfold.

8

Repeat steps 6–7 in the
opposite direction.

9

Unfold.

10

Bring the corner
to the line.

11

Unfold.

12

Repeat steps 10–11 in
the opposite direction.

13

Fold and unfold.

14

Bring the dots to the lines.

15

Bring the dot to the line.

16

1. Unfold.
2. Unfold.
3. Valley-fold.

17

Fold along the creases.

18

Fold along the crease.

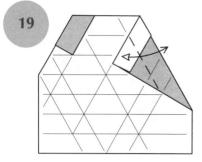

19

Fold and unfold along
a hidden crease.

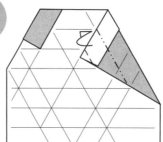

20

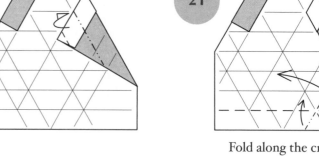

21

Fold along the creases.

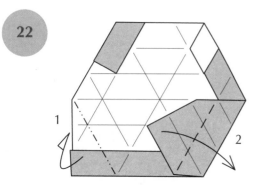

22

1. Fold along the crease.
2. Fold along a hidden crease.

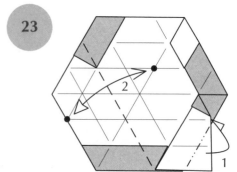

23

1. Tuck inside.
2. Fold and unfold.

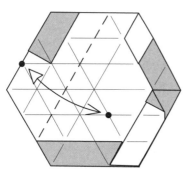

24

Fold and unfold.

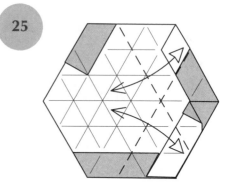

25

Fold and unfold.

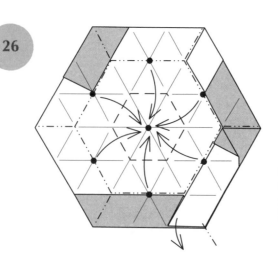

26

Collapse along the creases. The
dots will go to the center as the
model becomes 3D. Note the
larger corner at the bottom right.

Moon's View

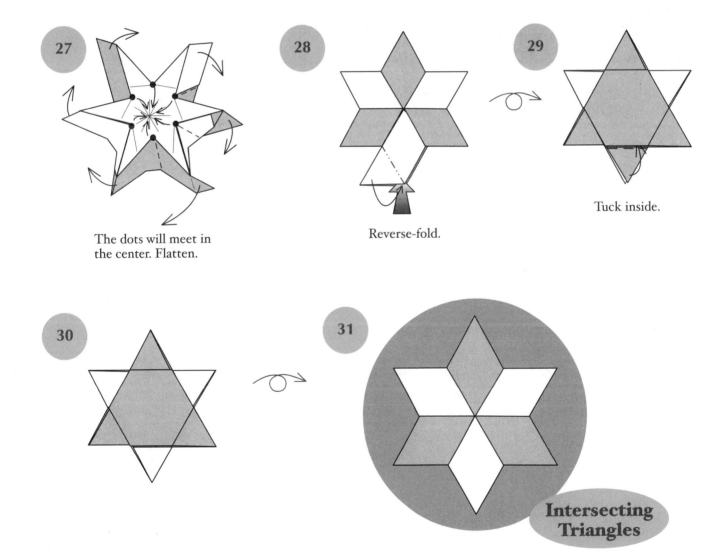

27 The dots will meet in the center. Flatten.

28 Reverse-fold.

29 Tuck inside.

30

31 Intersecting Triangles

Kaleidoscopic Star

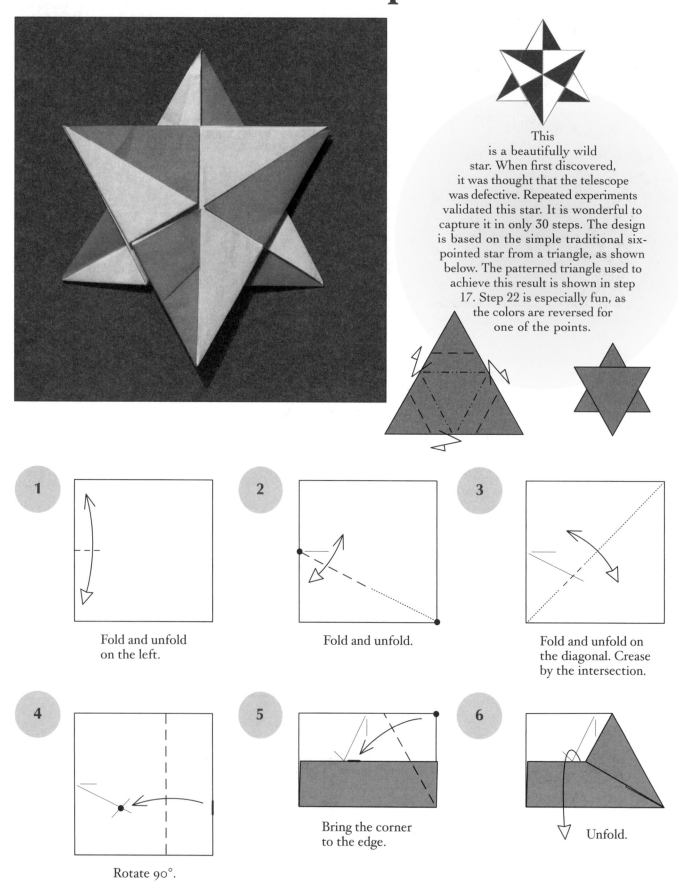

This is a beautifully wild star. When first discovered, it was thought that the telescope was defective. Repeated experiments validated this star. It is wonderful to capture it in only 30 steps. The design is based on the simple traditional six-pointed star from a triangle, as shown below. The patterned triangle used to achieve this result is shown in step 17. Step 22 is especially fun, as the colors are reversed for one of the points.

1

Fold and unfold on the left.

2

Fold and unfold.

3

Fold and unfold on the diagonal. Crease by the intersection.

4

Rotate 90°.

5

Bring the corner to the edge.

6

Unfold.

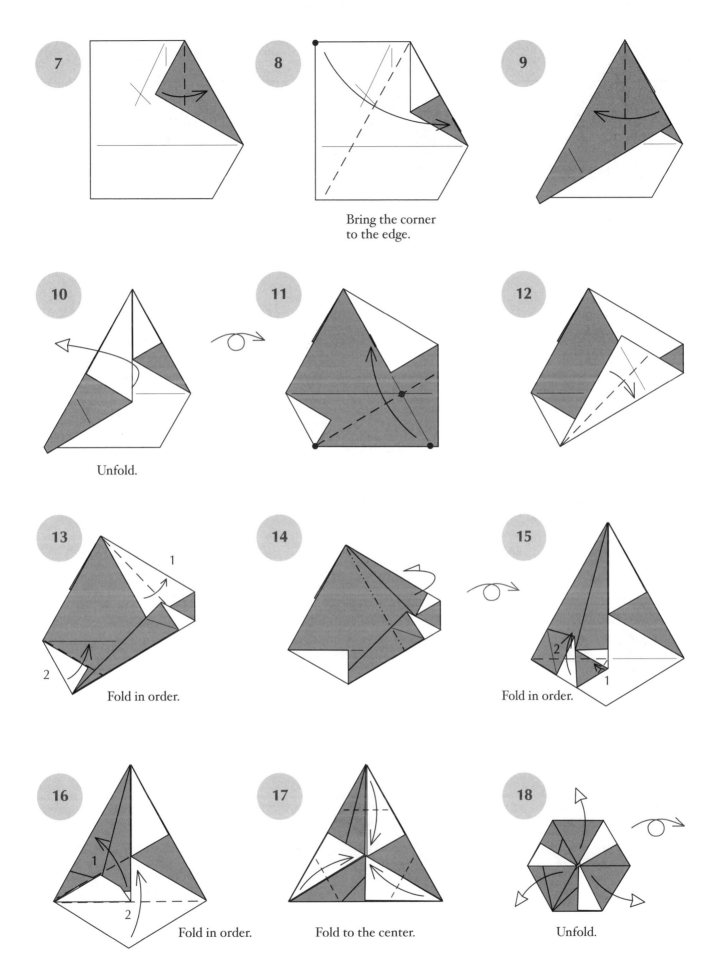

7

8

Bring the corner
to the edge.

9

10

Unfold.

11

12

13

Fold in order.

14

15

Fold in order.

16

Fold in order.

17

Fold to the center.

18

Unfold.

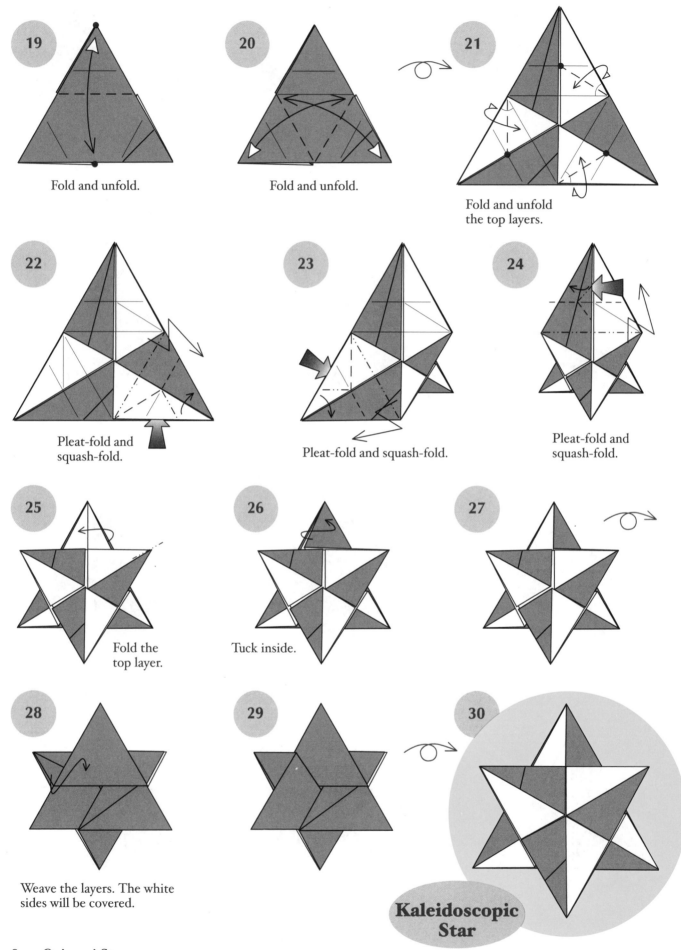

19 Fold and unfold.

20 Fold and unfold.

21 Fold and unfold the top layers.

22 Pleat-fold and squash-fold.

23 Pleat-fold and squash-fold.

24 Pleat-fold and squash-fold.

25 Fold the top layer.

26 Tuck inside.

27

28 Weave the layers. The white sides will be covered.

29

30 Kaleidoscopic Star

Radioactive Star

The Radioactive Star has a wild interior. It takes 31 steps to set up the patterned hexagon that will collapse into this star. The part that is especially fun for the folder, when making these colorful stars, is that much of the folding process is far from routine, such as steps 15 onward for this model. Nimble fingers are required to fold this successfully. To protect you from its dangerous rays, it is recommended that you fold it with lead gloves.

When you have captured all ten stars in this section, you will become Master of six-pointed stars.

1

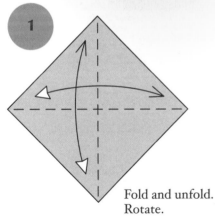

Fold and unfold.
Rotate.

2

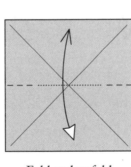

Fold and unfold
on the edges.

3

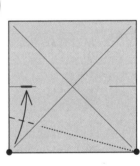

Bring the corner
to the crease.

4

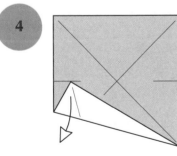

Unfold.

5

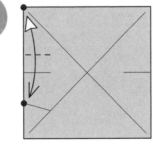

Fold and unfold.
Rotate 180°.

6

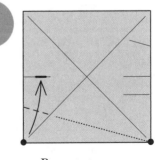

Repeat steps 3–5.

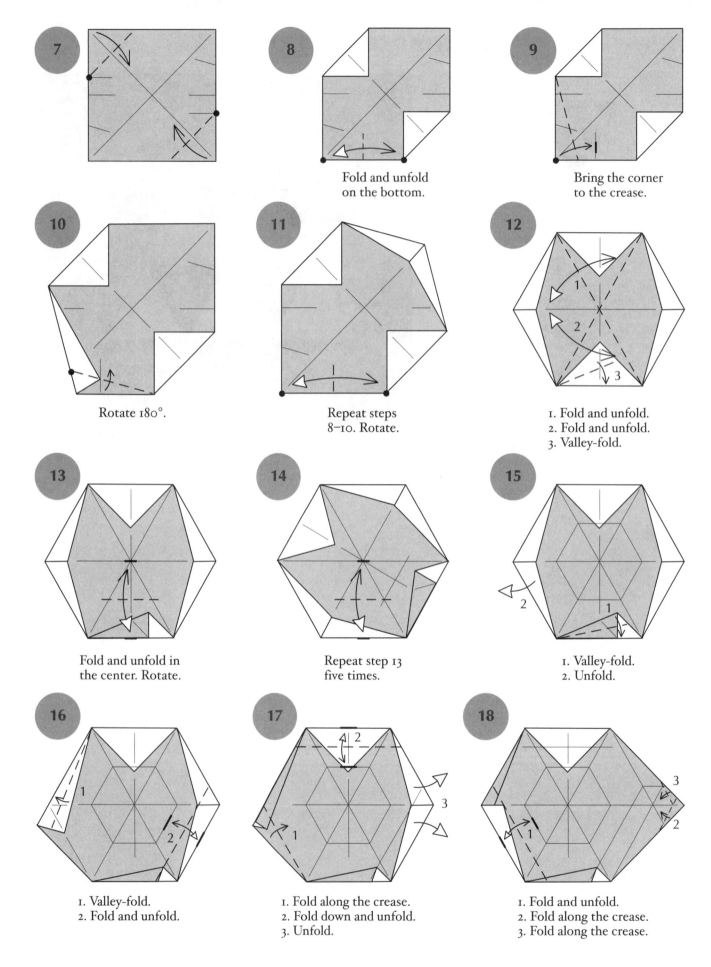

7

8 Fold and unfold on the bottom.

9 Bring the corner to the crease.

10 Rotate 180°.

11 Repeat steps 8–10. Rotate.

12
1. Fold and unfold.
2. Fold and unfold.
3. Valley-fold.

13 Fold and unfold in the center. Rotate.

14 Repeat step 13 five times.

15
1. Valley-fold.
2. Unfold.

16
1. Valley-fold.
2. Fold and unfold.

17
1. Fold along the crease.
2. Fold down and unfold.
3. Unfold.

18
1. Fold and unfold.
2. Fold along the crease.
3. Fold along the crease.

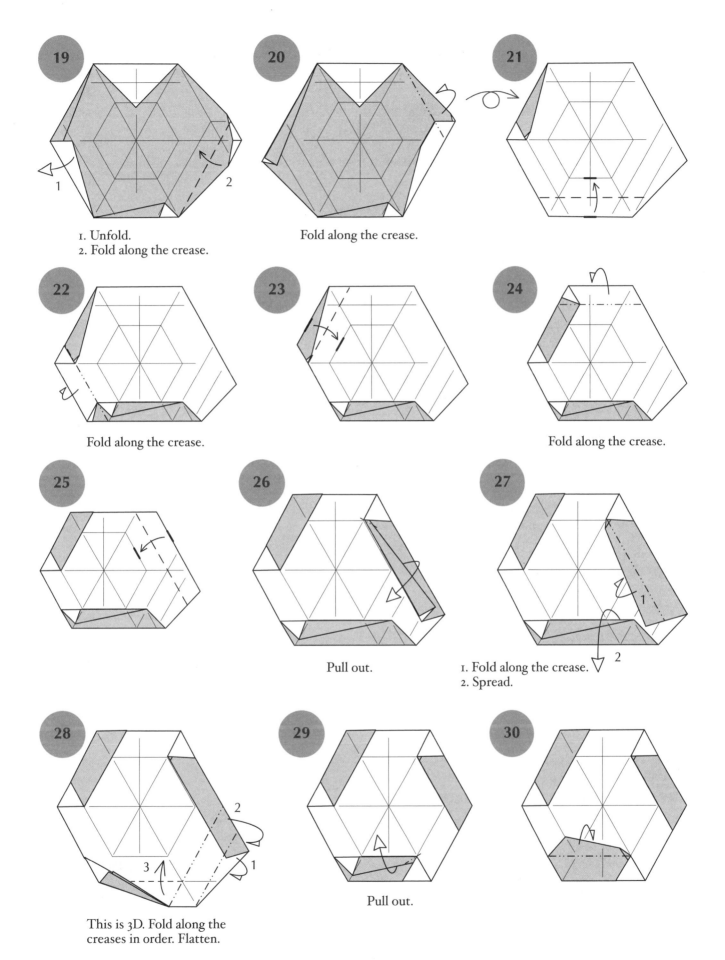

19

1. Unfold.
2. Fold along the crease.

20

Fold along the crease.

21

22

Fold along the crease.

23

24

Fold along the crease.

25

26

Pull out.

27

1. Fold along the crease.
2. Spread.

28

This is 3D. Fold along the creases in order. Flatten.

29

Pull out.

30

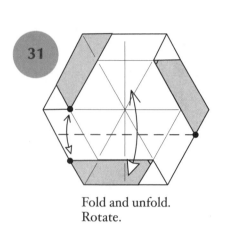

31

Fold and unfold.
Rotate.

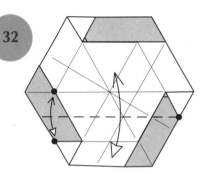

32

Repeat step 31
five times.

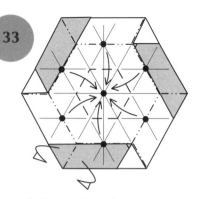

33

Collapse along the creases.
The dots will go to the center
as the model becomes 3D.

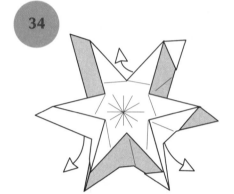

34

This is 3D. Pull out on
the three sides which
are mostly white.

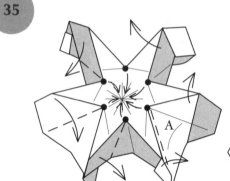

35

The dots will meet in
the center. Flatten.

This is a
side view of
region A.

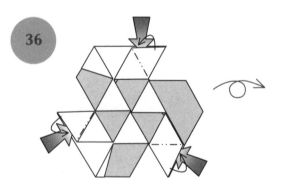

36

Reverse folds.

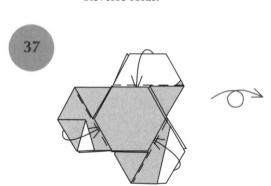

37

Tuck inside.

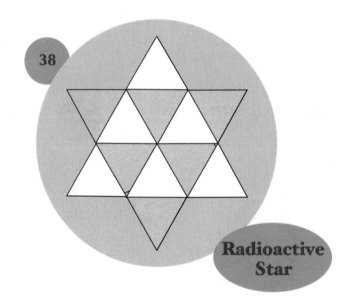

38

**Radioactive
Star**

Stars with Seven Points

Stars with seven points are rare, but as the universe contains billions of stars, many of these can be found. Due to the space in this volume, as opposed to the space in space, only one star appears here.

Seven-Pointed Star

The square is folded into a heptagon to form the radially symmetrical seven-pointed star. The heptagon is shown in step 14 and is shaped into an asterisk in step 31. Like all the stars in this volume, the folding process is under 40 steps. I recommend that you design some seven-pointed stars.

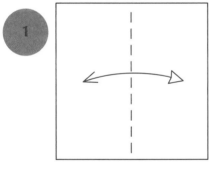

1

Fold and unfold.

2

Fold and unfold in half twice, on the bottom.

3

Fold and unfold on the left.

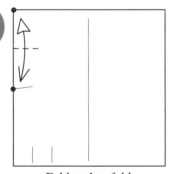

4

Fold and unfold on the left.

5

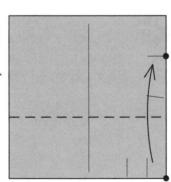

6

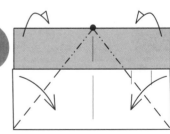

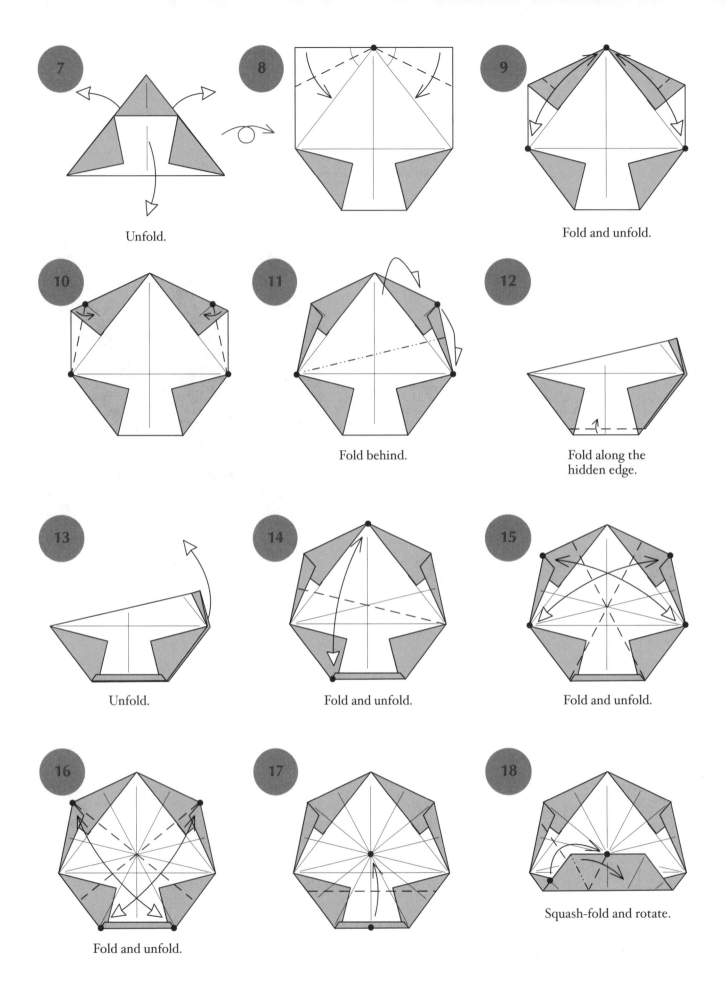

7 Unfold.

8

9 Fold and unfold.

10

11 Fold behind.

12 Fold along the hidden edge.

13 Unfold.

14 Fold and unfold.

15 Fold and unfold.

16 Fold and unfold.

17

18 Squash-fold and rotate.

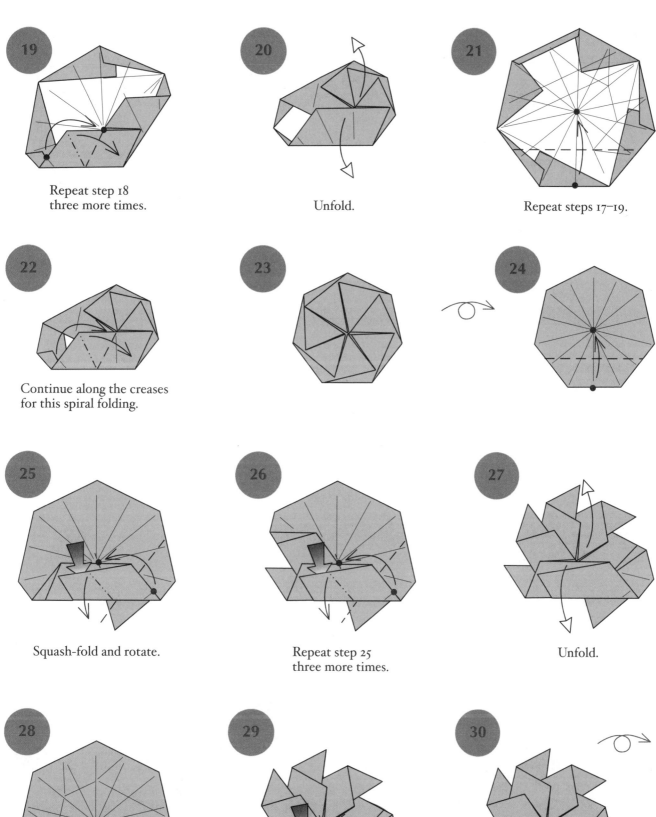

19

Repeat step 18
three more times.

20

Unfold.

21

Repeat steps 17–19.

22

Continue along the creases
for this spiral folding.

23

24

25

Squash-fold and rotate.

26

Repeat step 25
three more times.

27

Unfold.

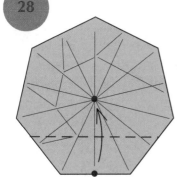

28

Repeat steps 24–26.

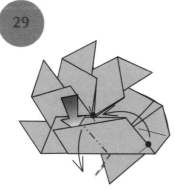

29

Continue along the creases
for this spiral folding.

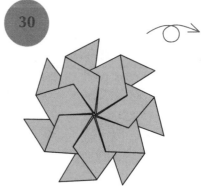

30

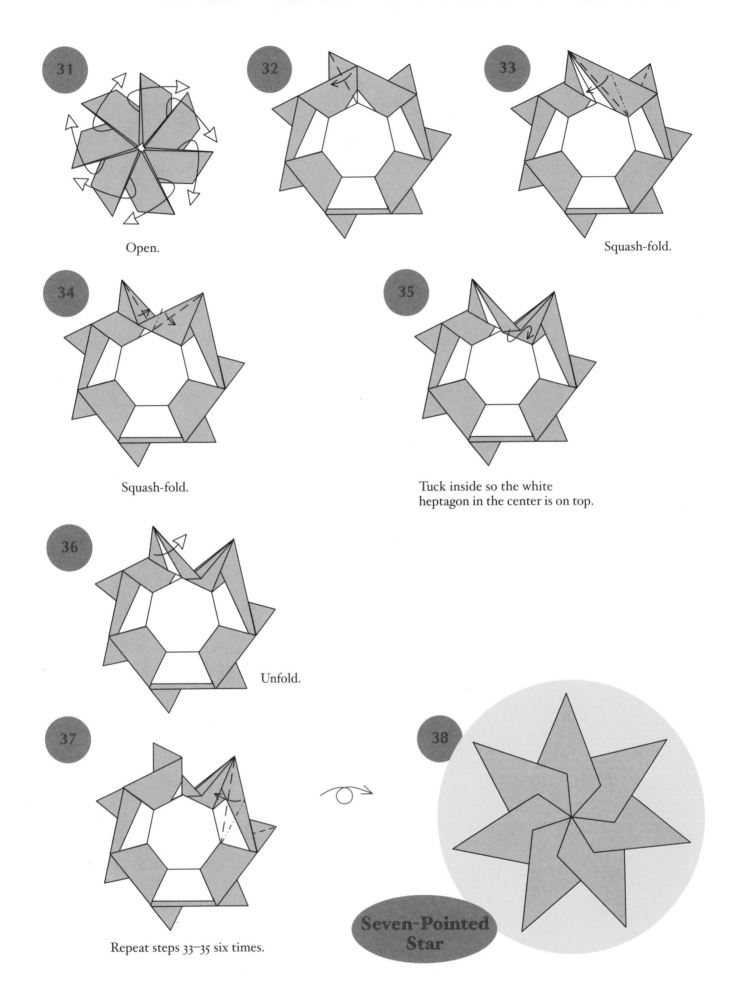

31 Open.

32

33 Squash-fold.

34 Squash-fold.

35 Tuck inside so the white heptagon in the center is on top.

36 Unfold.

37 Repeat steps 33–35 six times.

38 Seven-Pointed Star

Stars with Eight Points

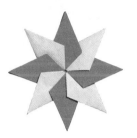

Stars with eight points are more complex and further evolved. They come in varied shapes and colorful patterns. Square and octagonal symmetry is used. Capturing these shows a higher level of skill on your way to becoming the Master of the Universe.

——— Eight-Pointed Star ———

Designed by Russell Cashdollar

This Eight-Pointed Star uses octagonal symmetry. The square is folded into an octagon, as shown in step 7. The spiral interior shows its dynamic nature.

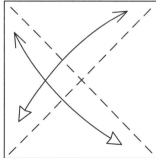

Fold and unfold.

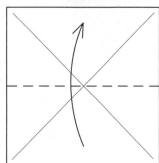

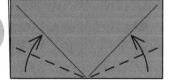

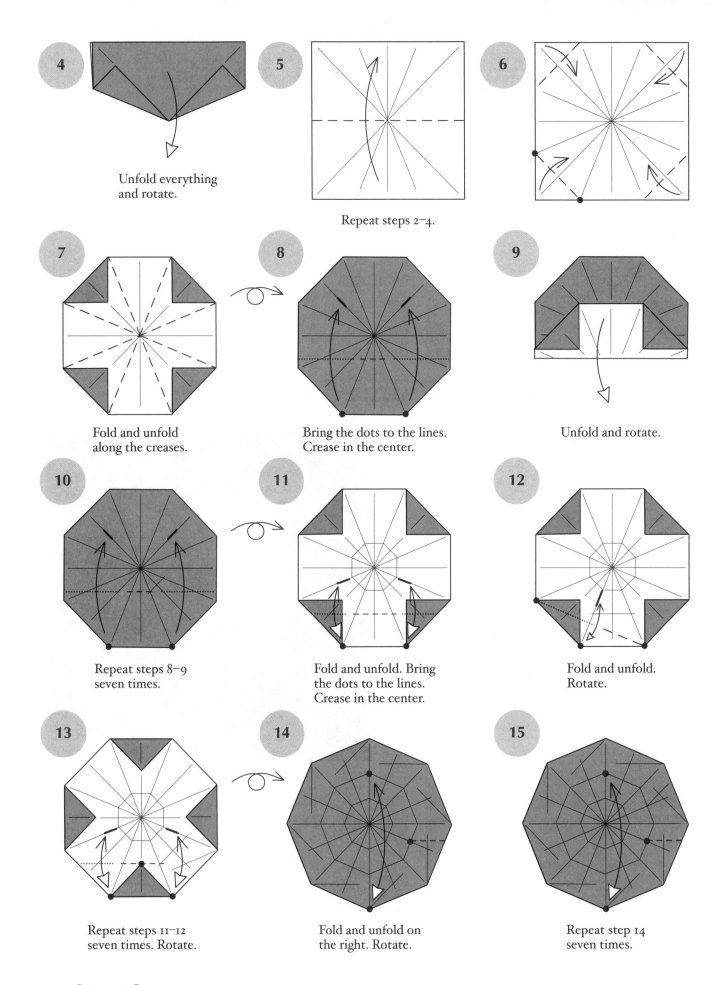

4 Unfold everything and rotate.

5 Repeat steps 2–4.

6

7 Fold and unfold along the creases.

8 Bring the dots to the lines. Crease in the center.

9 Unfold and rotate.

10 Repeat steps 8–9 seven times.

11 Fold and unfold. Bring the dots to the lines. Crease in the center.

12 Fold and unfold. Rotate.

13 Repeat steps 11–12 seven times. Rotate.

14 Fold and unfold on the right. Rotate.

15 Repeat step 14 seven times.

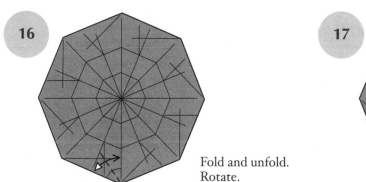

16 Fold and unfold. Rotate.

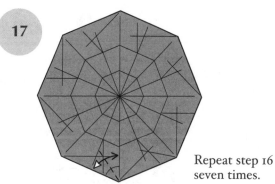

17 Repeat step 16 seven times.

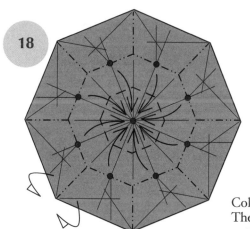

18 Collapse along the creases. The dots will go to the center as the model becomes 3D.

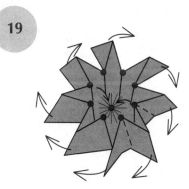

19 The dots will meet in the center. Flatten.

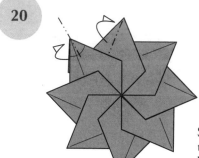

20 Squash-fold along the creases. Tuck behind inner layers.

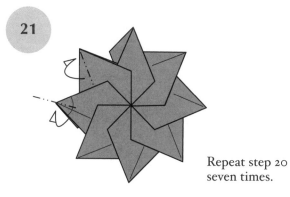

21 Repeat step 20 seven times.

22

Eight-Pointed Star

Twirling Star

The Twirling Star is a classic design often used in quilts. It can also be called the Colorful Woven Eight-Pointed Star. This model is based on overlapping squares, as shown in step 9.

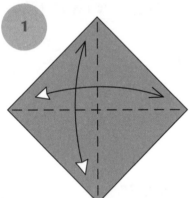

1

Fold and unfold.

2

Fold and unfold.

3

Fold to the center and unfold.

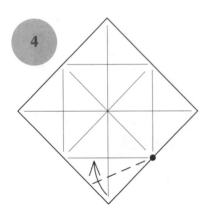

4

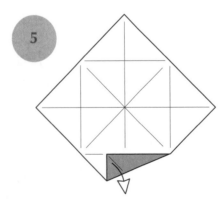

5

Unfold.

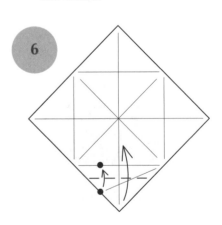

6

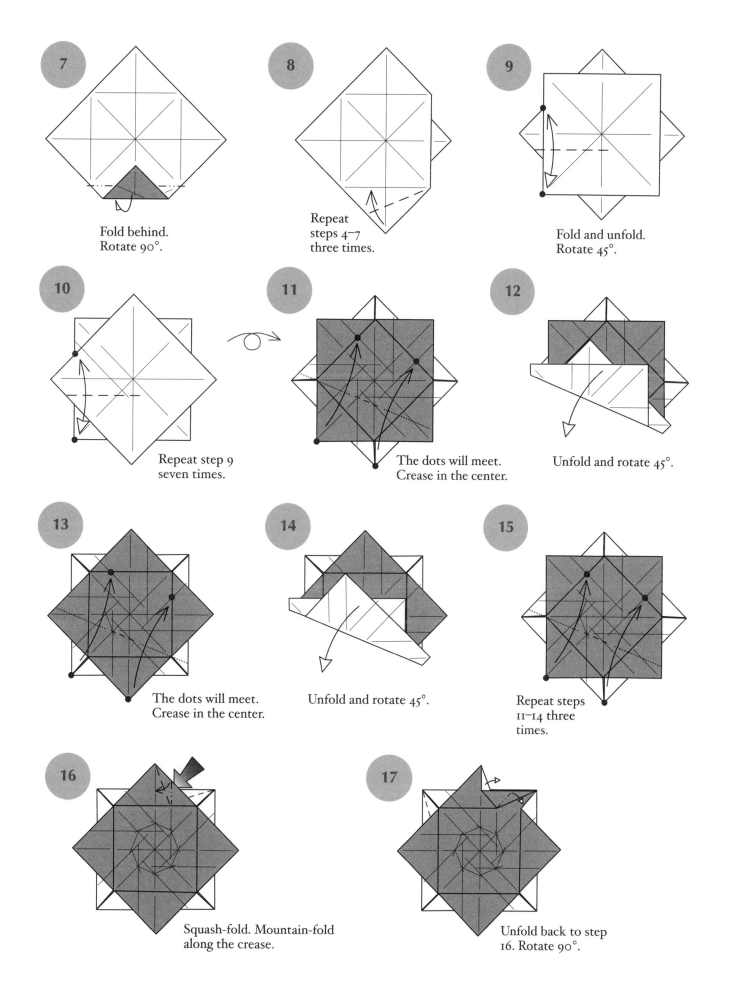

7 Fold behind. Rotate 90°.

8 Repeat steps 4–7 three times.

9 Fold and unfold. Rotate 45°.

10 Repeat step 9 seven times.

11 The dots will meet. Crease in the center.

12 Unfold and rotate 45°.

13 The dots will meet. Crease in the center.

14 Unfold and rotate 45°.

15 Repeat steps 11–14 three times.

16 Squash-fold. Mountain-fold along the crease.

17 Unfold back to step 16. Rotate 90°.

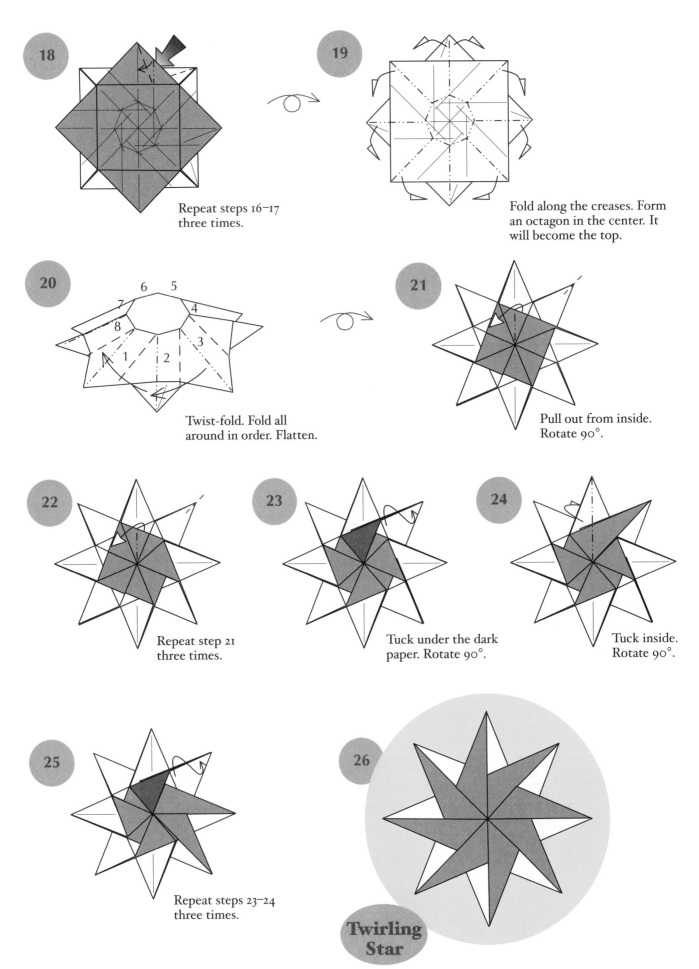

18

Repeat steps 16–17 three times.

19

Fold along the creases. Form an octagon in the center. It will become the top.

20

6 5
7 4
8 3
1 2

Twist-fold. Fold all around in order. Flatten.

21

Pull out from inside. Rotate 90°.

22

Repeat step 21 three times.

23

Tuck under the dark paper. Rotate 90°.

24

Tuck inside. Rotate 90°.

25

Repeat steps 23–24 three times.

26

Twirling Star

Sun

We come to our closest star and the one that has the greatest impact on us. This star defines our day, night, and year. Yet, unlike all the other stars, this is the one you don't want to look at. If you have reached this stage in your starry collection, it is only because this one shines upon you every day. If you have ever wondered how the Sun was formed, simply follow these instructions. Creating this at your whim will give you far-reaching powers; however, to protect yourself from its unbounded energy, only fold it at night.

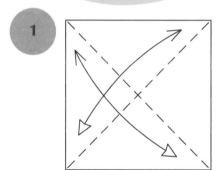

Fold and unfold.

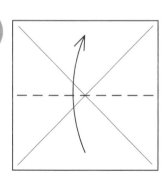

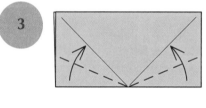

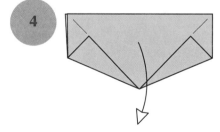

Unfold everything and rotate.

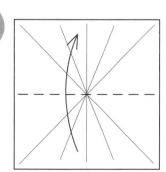

Repeat steps 2–4.

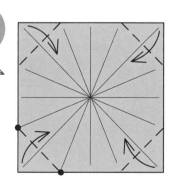

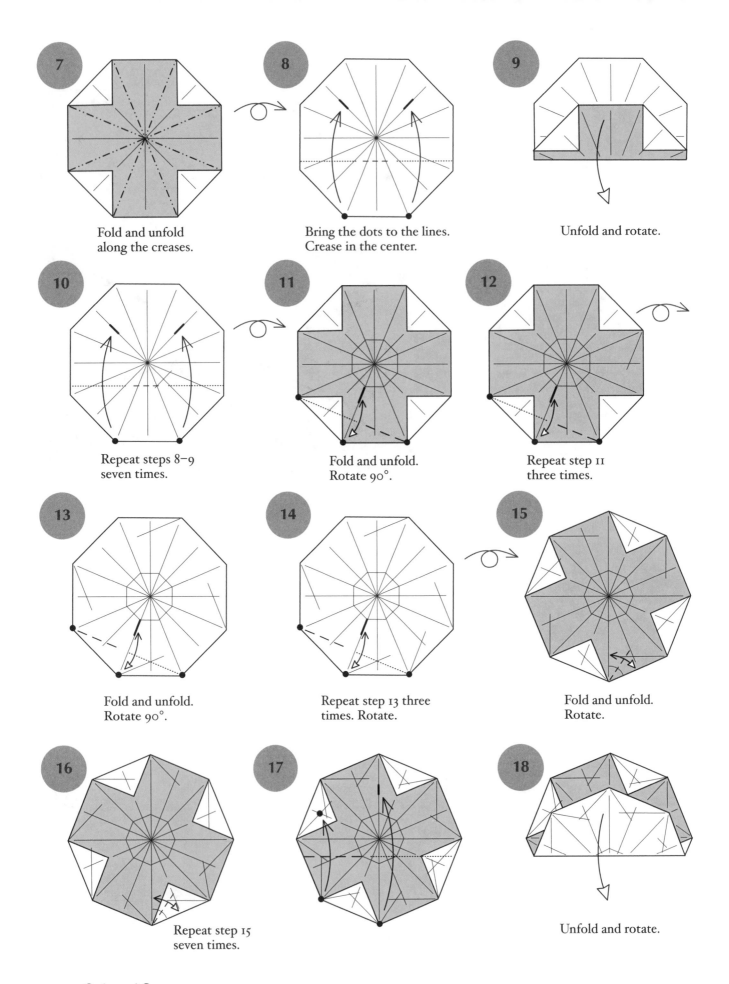

7 Fold and unfold along the creases.

8 Bring the dots to the lines. Crease in the center.

9 Unfold and rotate.

10 Repeat steps 8–9 seven times.

11 Fold and unfold. Rotate 90°.

12 Repeat step 11 three times.

13 Fold and unfold. Rotate 90°.

14 Repeat step 13 three times. Rotate.

15 Fold and unfold. Rotate.

16 Repeat step 15 seven times.

17

18 Unfold and rotate.

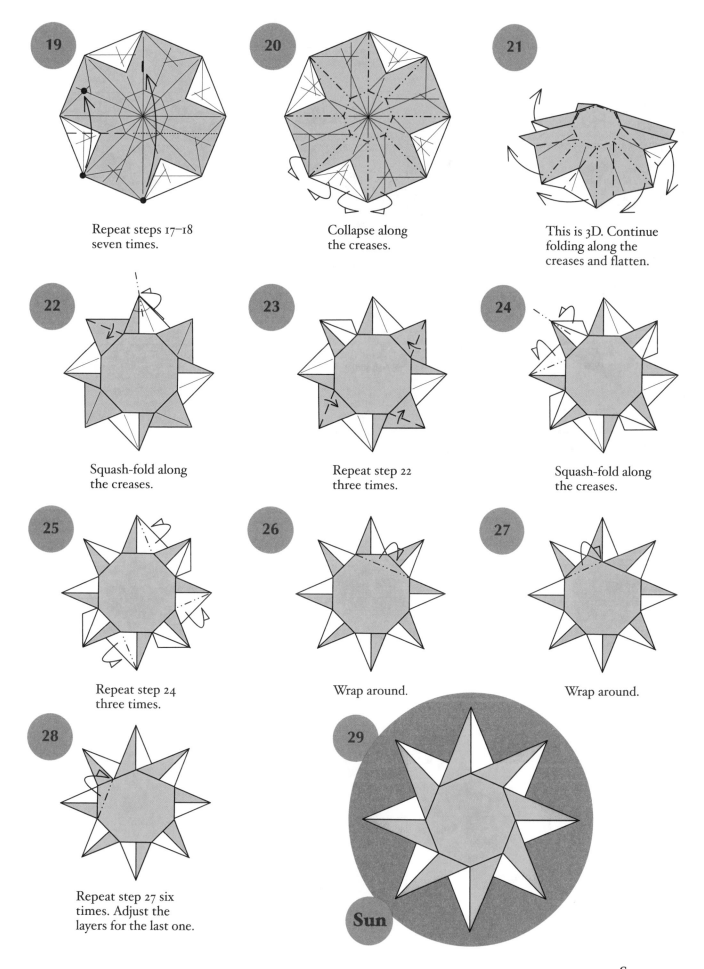

19 Repeat steps 17–18 seven times.

20 Collapse along the creases.

21 This is 3D. Continue folding along the creases and flatten.

22 Squash-fold along the creases.

23 Repeat step 22 three times.

24 Squash-fold along the creases.

25 Repeat step 24 three times.

26 Wrap around.

27 Wrap around.

28 Repeat step 27 six times. Adjust the layers for the last one.

29 **Sun**

Colorful Eight-Pointed Star

Designed by Russell Cashdollar

The effective, overlapping colorful pattern shows the immense energy radiated by this star. This star is based on the Eight-Pointed Star formed from an octagonal structure. The patterned octagon used to achieve this star is shown in step 26.

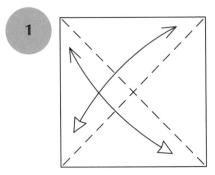

Fold and unfold.

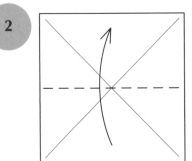

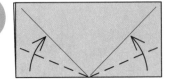

Repeat steps 2–4.

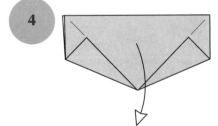

Unfold everything and rotate.

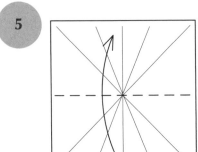

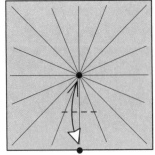

Fold and unfold.
Rotate 90°.

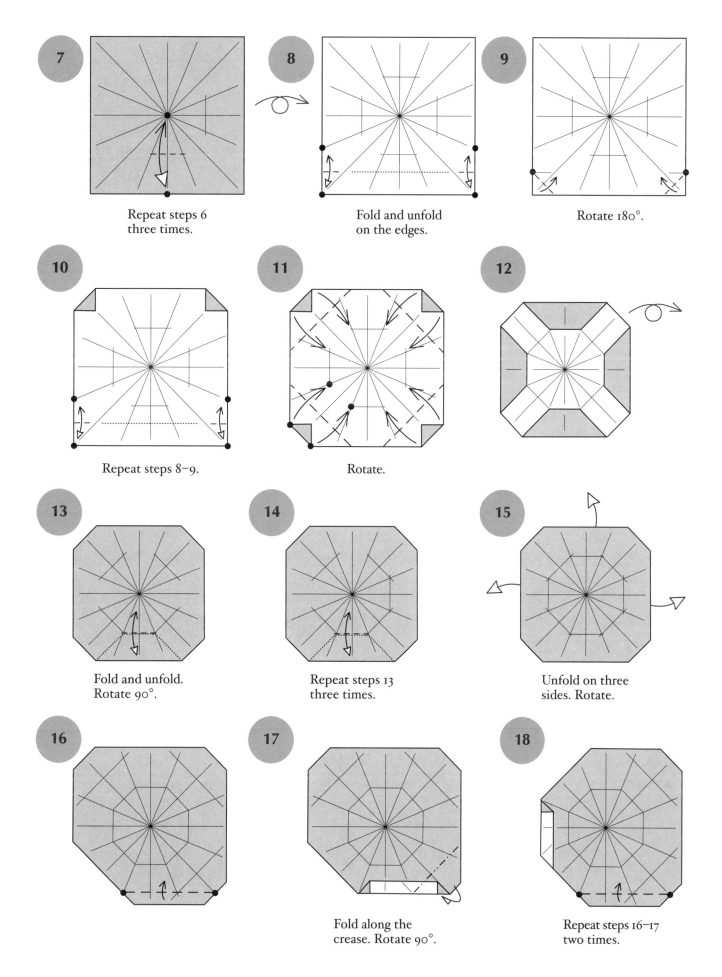

7 Repeat steps 6 three times.

8 Fold and unfold on the edges.

9 Rotate 180°.

10 Repeat steps 8–9.

11 Rotate.

12

13 Fold and unfold. Rotate 90°.

14 Repeat steps 13 three times.

15 Unfold on three sides. Rotate.

16

17 Fold along the crease. Rotate 90°.

18 Repeat steps 16–17 two times.

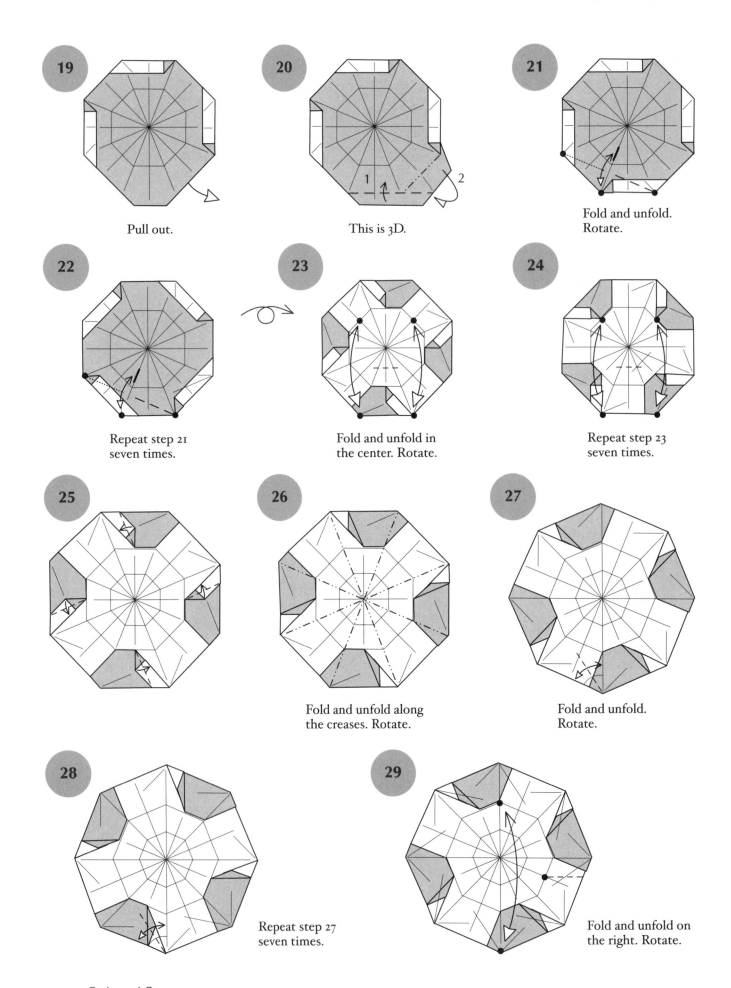

19

Pull out.

20

This is 3D.

21

Fold and unfold.
Rotate.

22

Repeat step 21
seven times.

23

Fold and unfold in
the center. Rotate.

24

Repeat step 23
seven times.

25

26

Fold and unfold along
the creases. Rotate.

27

Fold and unfold.
Rotate.

28

Repeat step 27
seven times.

29

Fold and unfold on
the right. Rotate.

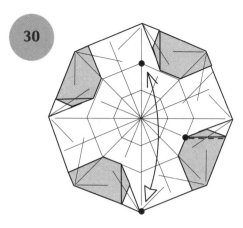

30

Repeat step 29
seven times.

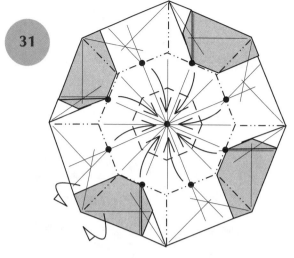

31

Collapse along the creases.
The dots will go to the center
as the model becomes 3D.

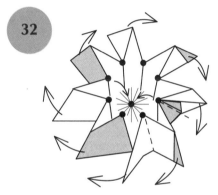

32

The dots will meet in
the center. Flatten.

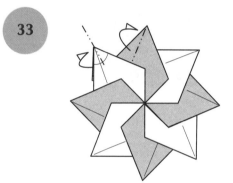

33

Squash-fold along
the creases. Tuck
behind inner layers.

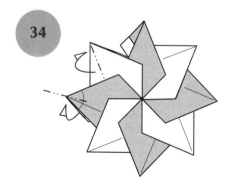

34

Repeat step 33
seven times.

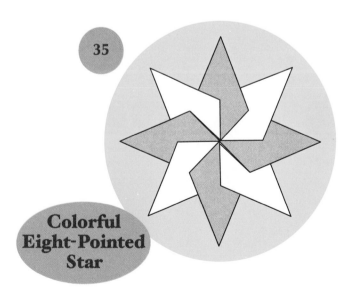

35

**Colorful
Eight-Pointed
Star**

Eight-Pointed Propeller

This star is double-sided. It can spin at great speeds as it travels throughout its galaxy. Once captured, you will have the power to also travel quickly throughout the galaxy. This model begins with the famous Waterbomb Base shown in step 7.

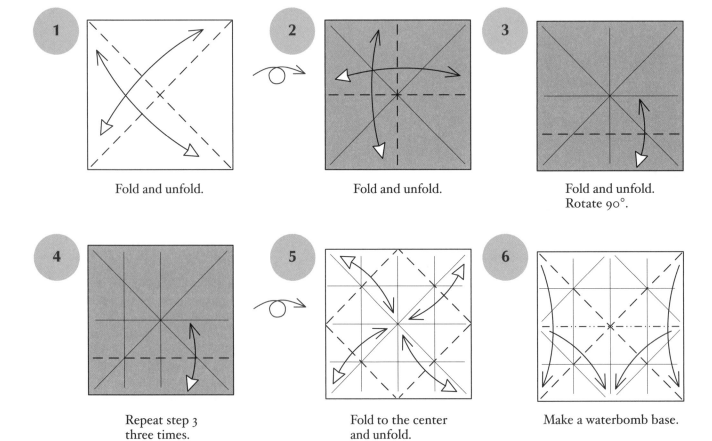

1. Fold and unfold.

2. Fold and unfold.

3. Fold and unfold. Rotate 90°.

4. Repeat step 3 three times.

5. Fold to the center and unfold.

6. Make a waterbomb base.

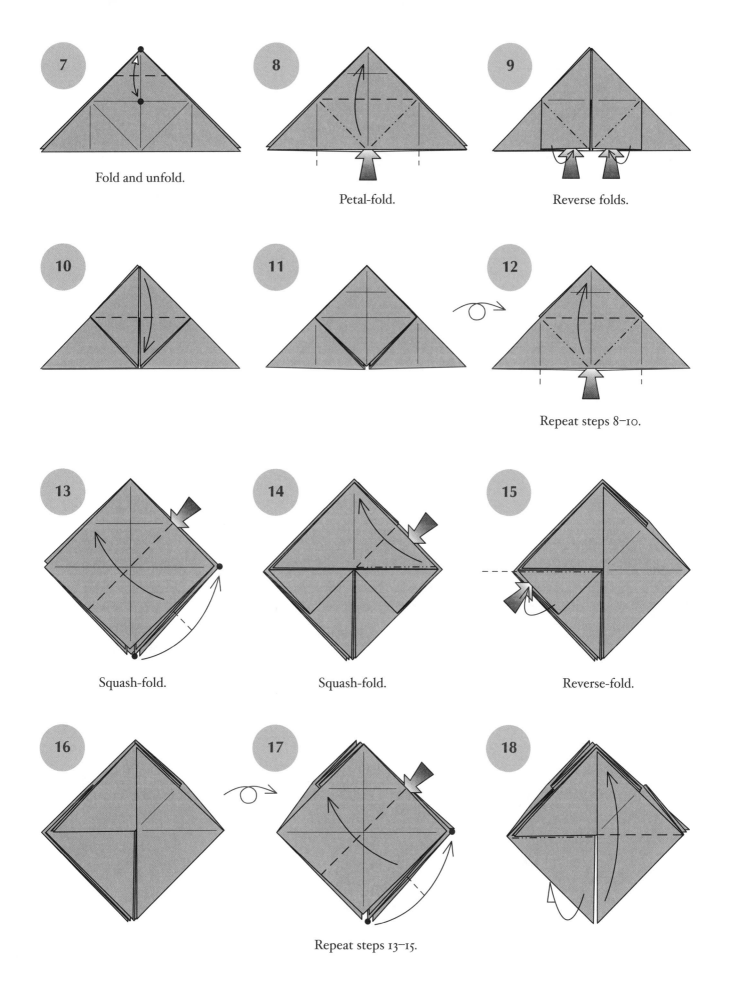

7 Fold and unfold.

8 Petal-fold.

9 Reverse folds.

10

11

12 Repeat steps 8–10.

13 Squash-fold.

14 Squash-fold.

15 Reverse-fold.

16

17 Repeat steps 13–15.

18

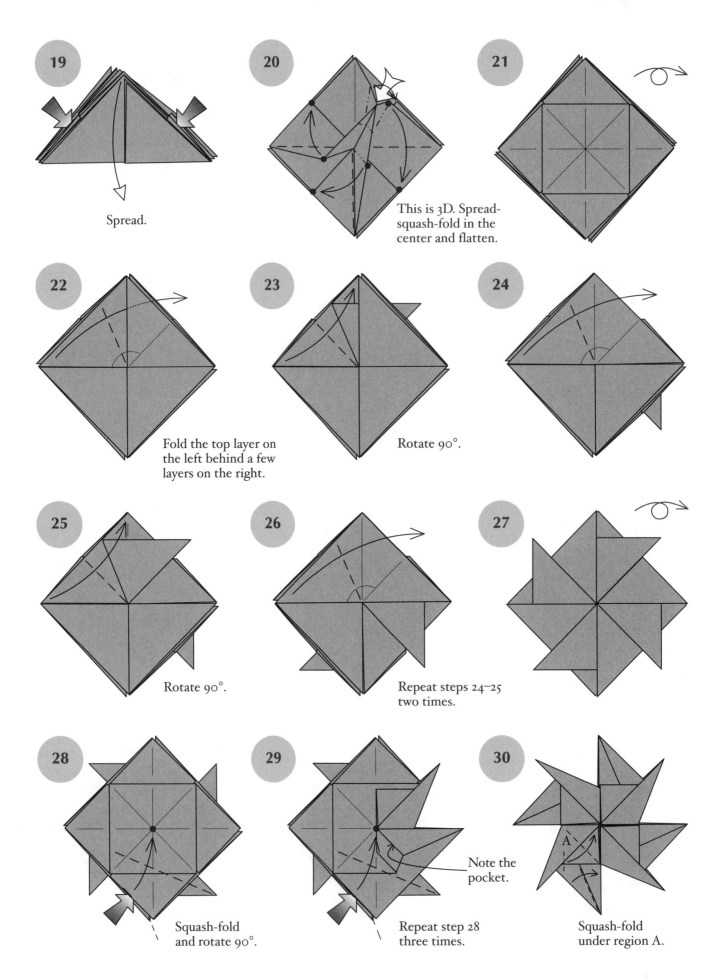

19 Spread.

20 This is 3D. Spread-squash-fold in the center and flatten.

21

22 Fold the top layer on the left behind a few layers on the right.

23 Rotate 90°.

24

25 Rotate 90°.

26 Repeat steps 24–25 two times.

27

28 Squash-fold and rotate 90°.

29 Note the pocket. Repeat step 28 three times.

30 Squash-fold under region A.

Journey of the Eight-Pointed Stars

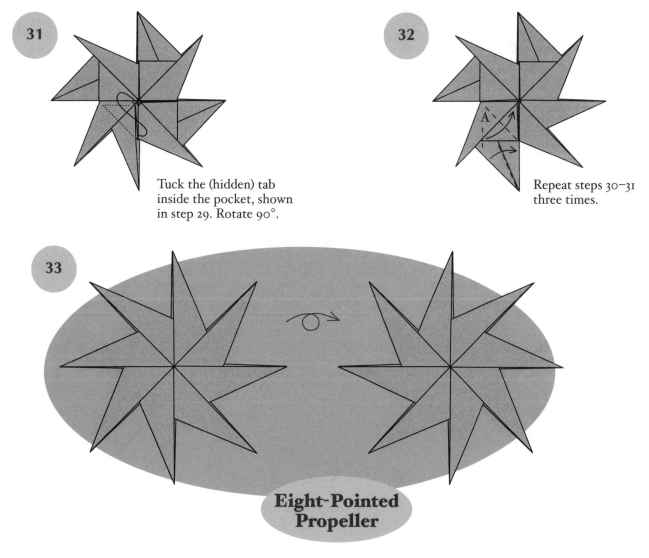

31 Tuck the (hidden) tab inside the pocket, shown in step 29. Rotate 90°.

32 Repeat steps 30–31 three times.

33

Eight-Pointed Propeller

Colorful Eight-Pointed Propeller

This colorful Propeller is a variation of the Eight-Pointed Propeller. The alternating colorful pattern allow these stars to reach higher speeds so they can move from galaxy to galaxy. Only the more evolved galaxies contain Colorful Eight-Pointed Stars. Capturing this star gives you the power to travel at super-speeds so you, too, can visit these galaxies.

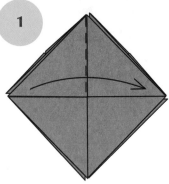

1 Begin with step 22 of the Eight-Pointed Propeller on page 106. Fold one flap.

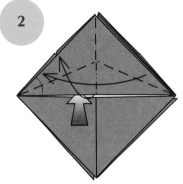

2 Lift some of the top layer up.

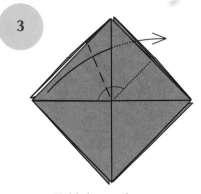

3 Fold the top layer on the left behind a few layers on the right.

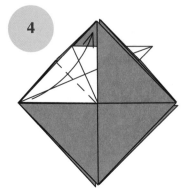

4 Rotate 90°.

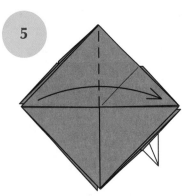

5 Fold one flap.

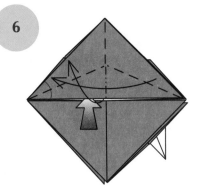

6 Lift some of the top layer up.

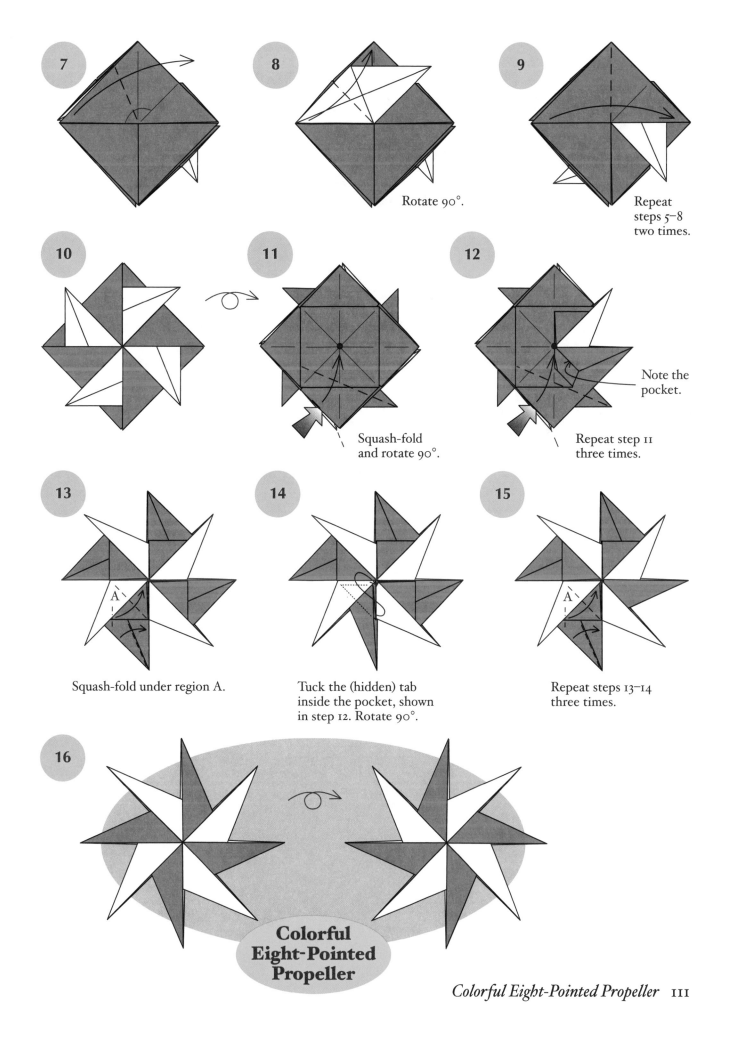

7

8

Rotate 90°.

9

Repeat steps 5–8 two times.

10

11

Squash-fold and rotate 90°.

12

Note the pocket.

Repeat step 11 three times.

13

Squash-fold under region A.

14

Tuck the (hidden) tab inside the pocket, shown in step 12. Rotate 90°.

15

Repeat steps 13–14 three times.

16

Colorful Eight-Pointed Propeller

Map Compass

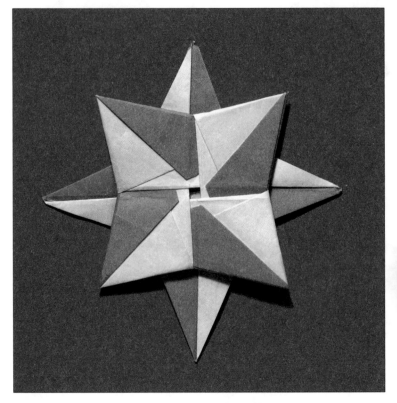

This wild model can also be called the Kaleidoscopic Eight-Pointed Star. It has square symmetry. Once captured, this rare star will give you the power of direction. You can buzz from galaxy to galaxy and not get lost. Once completed, along with all the previous stars, you will be the Master of all stars of eight points or less.

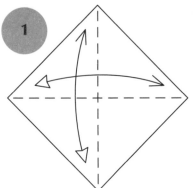

Fold and unfold.

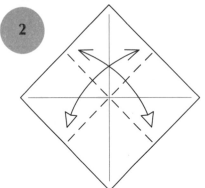

Fold and unfold.

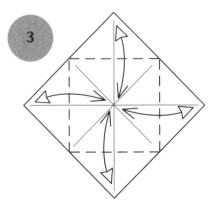

Fold to the center and unfold.

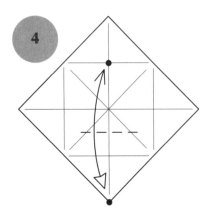

Fold and unfold in the center. Rotate 90°.

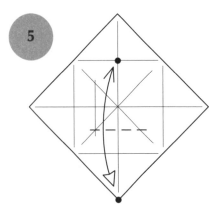

Repeat step 4 three times.

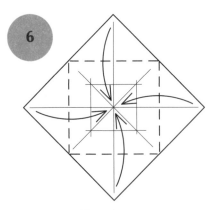

Fold to the center.

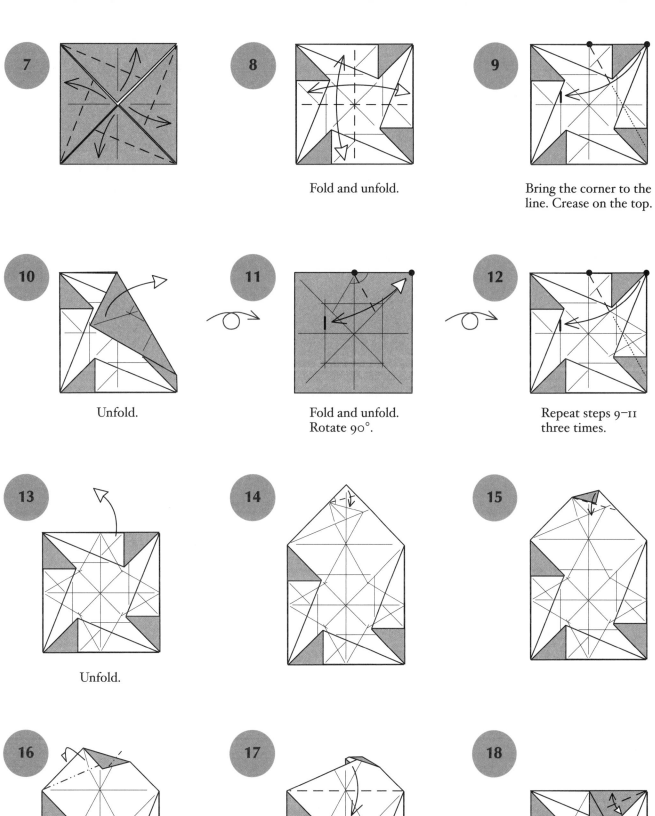

7

8

Fold and unfold.

9

Bring the corner to the line. Crease on the top.

10

Unfold.

11

Fold and unfold. Rotate 90°.

12

Repeat steps 9–11 three times.

13

Unfold.

14

15

16

Fold behind with a little squash fold on the right.

17

18

Fold and unfold the top layer. Rotate 90°.

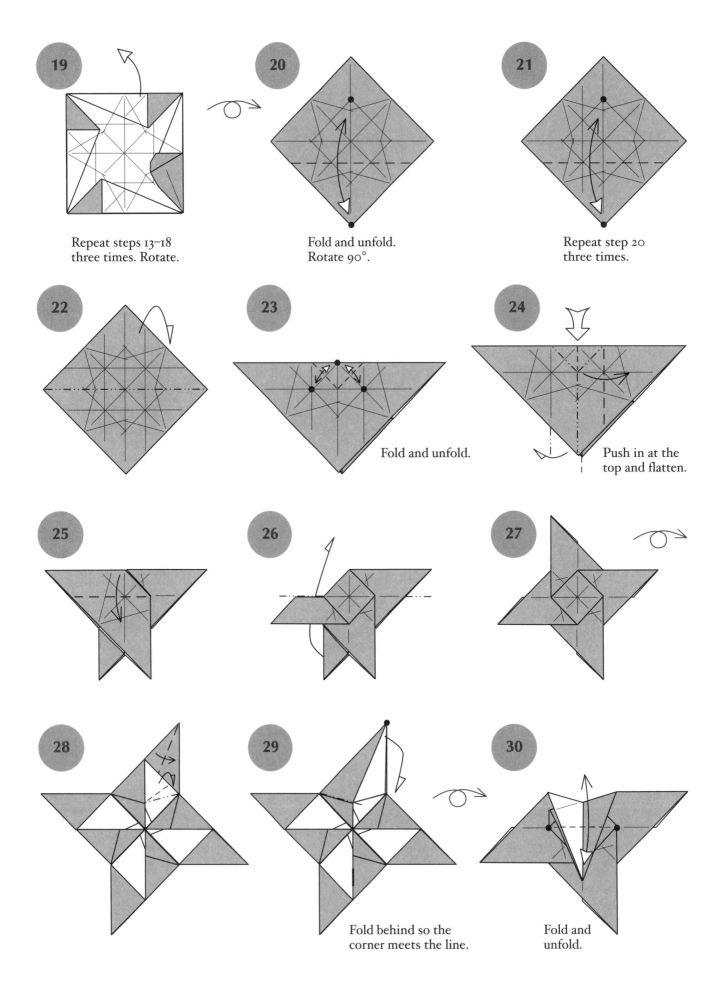

19 Repeat steps 13–18 three times. Rotate.

20 Fold and unfold. Rotate 90°.

21 Repeat step 20 three times.

22

23 Fold and unfold.

24 Push in at the top and flatten.

25

26

27

28

29 Fold behind so the corner meets the line.

30 Fold and unfold.

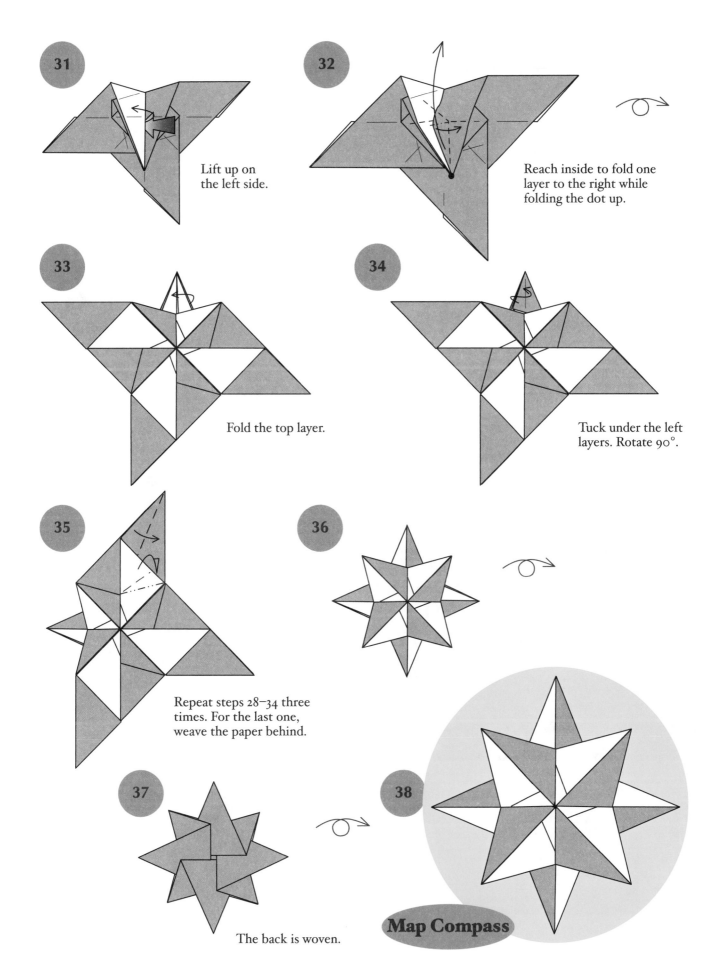

31 Lift up on the left side.

32 Reach inside to fold one layer to the right while folding the dot up.

33 Fold the top layer.

34 Tuck under the left layers. Rotate 90°.

35 Repeat steps 28–34 three times. For the last one, weave the paper behind.

36

37 The back is woven.

38

Map Compass

Stars with More Points

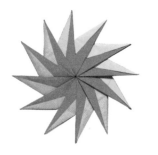

It took billions of years and billions of stars to evolve into the variety with more than eight points. These stars are the largest and brightest. Each star you fold will welcome you and tell you their celestial secrets, expanding your ever-growing powers.

Once you have captured all of these stars and arranged them in cosmic harmony you will then become Master of the Universe.

Ten-Pointed Star

This advanced Ten-Pointed Star is based on the decagon. The square is folded into a decagon in step 13. The folding process is similar to the Seven-Pointed Star. This star harbors many planets with super-intellegent life. However, it is best not to visit these planets as the creatures will only recognize you as a source of food, energy, or raw material.

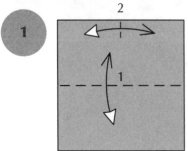

1. Fold and unfold.
2. Fold and unfold at the top.

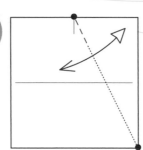

Fold and unfold by the top.

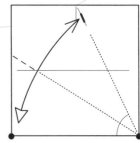

Fold and unfold on the left to bisect the angle.

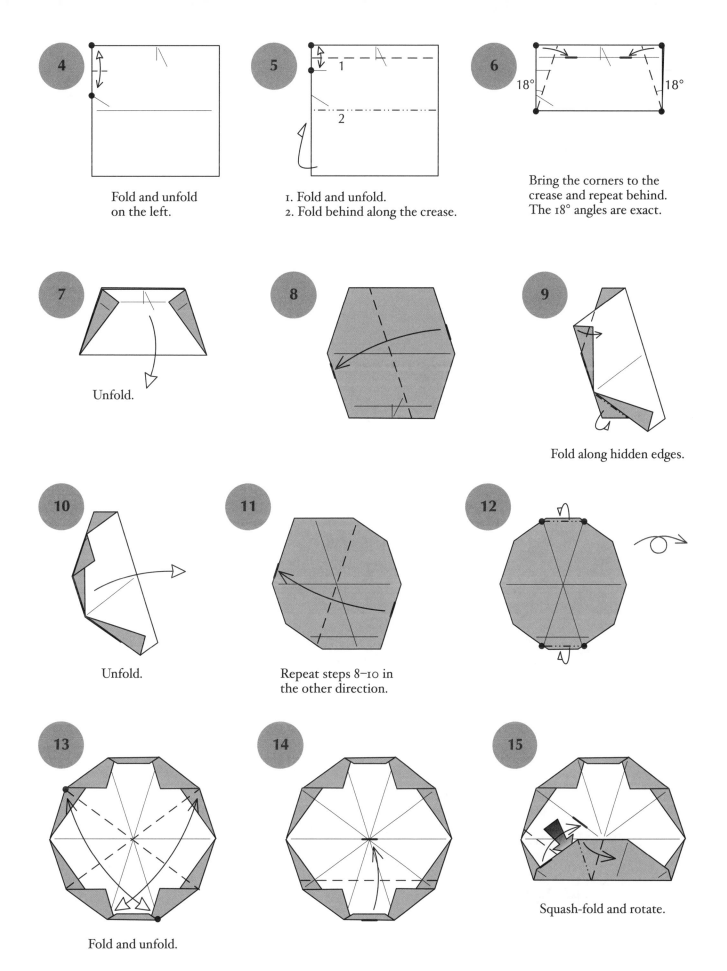

4 Fold and unfold on the left.

5
1. Fold and unfold.
2. Fold behind along the crease.

6 Bring the corners to the crease and repeat behind. The 18° angles are exact.

18°   18°

7 Unfold.

8

9 Fold along hidden edges.

10 Unfold.

11 Repeat steps 8–10 in the other direction.

12

13 Fold and unfold.

14

15 Squash-fold and rotate.

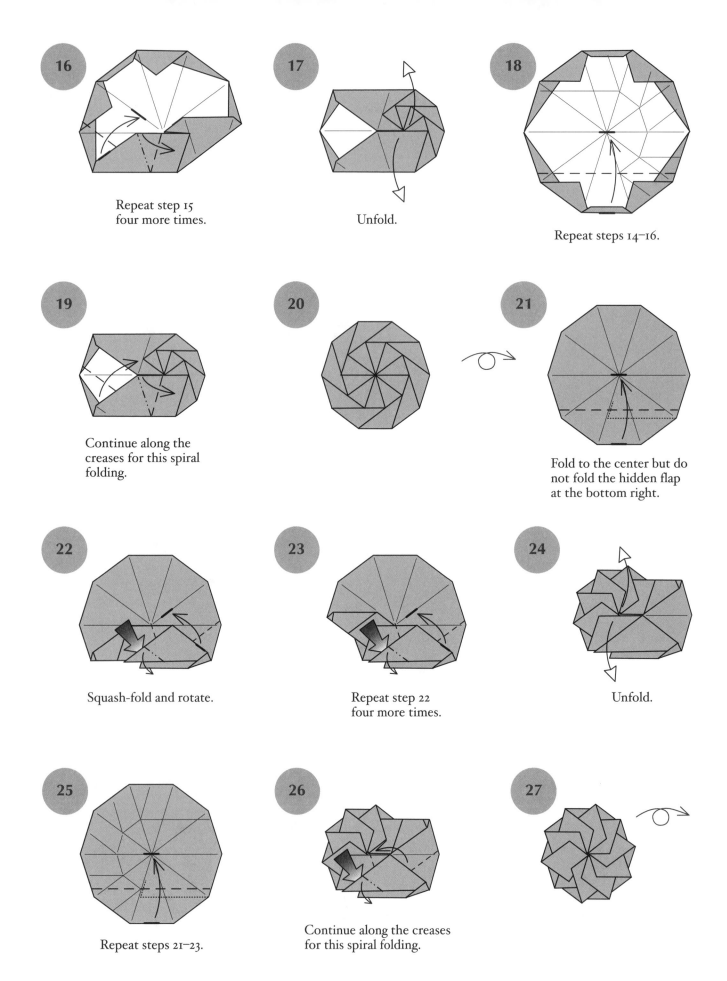

16

Repeat step 15
four more times.

17

Unfold.

18

Repeat steps 14–16.

19

Continue along the
creases for this spiral
folding.

20

21

Fold to the center but do
not fold the hidden flap
at the bottom right.

22

Squash-fold and rotate.

23

Repeat step 22
four more times.

24

Unfold.

25

Repeat steps 21–23.

26

Continue along the creases
for this spiral folding.

27

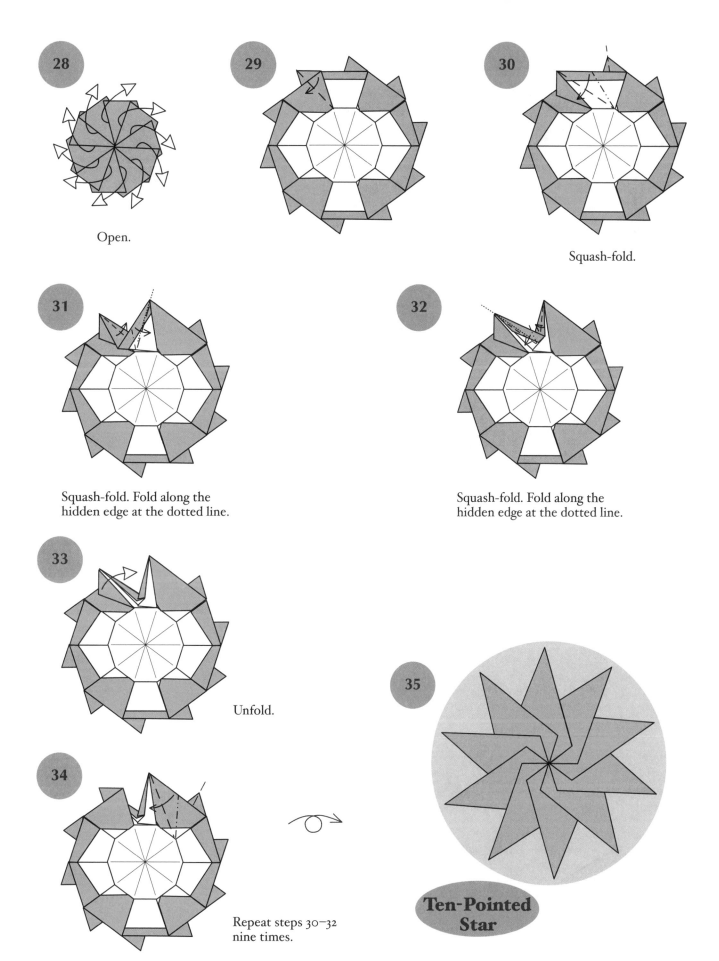

28 Open.

29

30 Squash-fold.

31 Squash-fold. Fold along the hidden edge at the dotted line.

32 Squash-fold. Fold along the hidden edge at the dotted line.

33 Unfold.

34 Repeat steps 30–32 nine times.

35

Ten-Pointed Star

Twelve-Pointed Star

This Twelve-Pointed Star is not as difficult to fold as some with fewer points. It is based on the hexagon. As with the Ten-Pointed Star, this star also has several planets with very intelligent creatures. These creatures are peaceful and would cause you no harm. However, they might find you fascinating as alien pets.

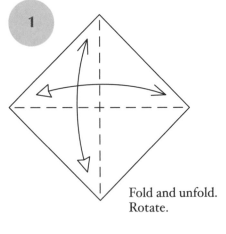

Fold and unfold.
Rotate.

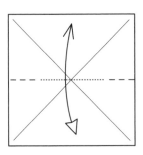

Fold and unfold
on the edges.

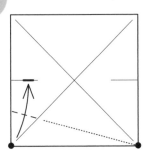

Bring the corner
to the crease.

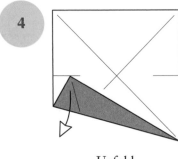

Unfold.

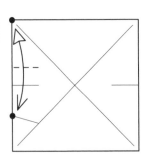

Fold and unfold.
Rotate 180°.

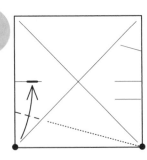

Repeat steps 3–5.

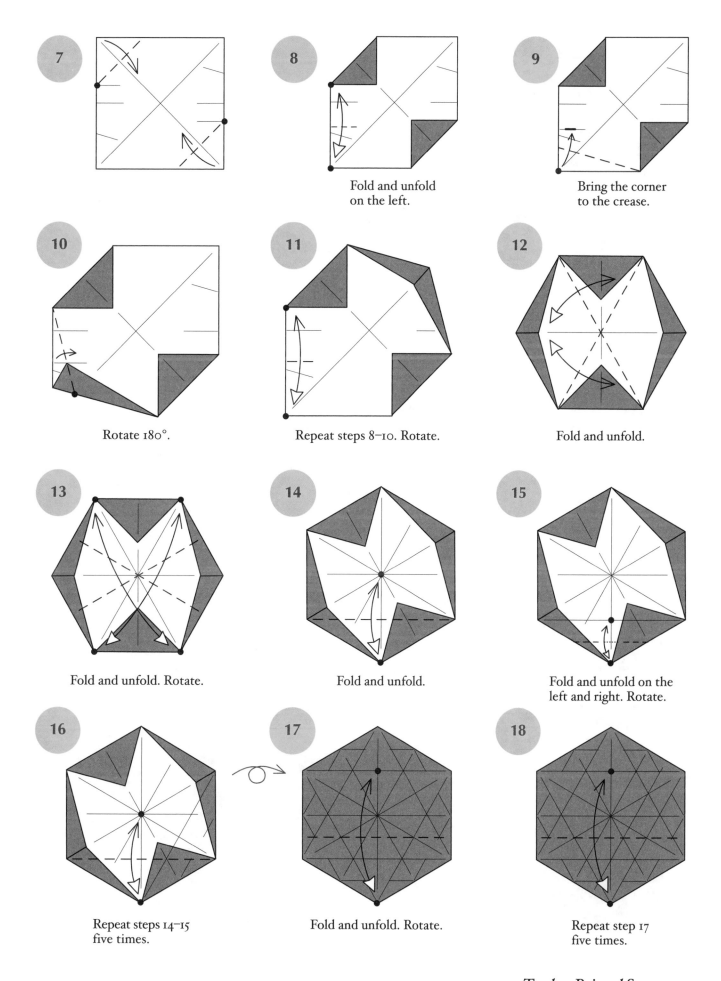

7

8 Fold and unfold
on the left.

9 Bring the corner
to the crease.

10 Rotate 180°.

11 Repeat steps 8–10. Rotate.

12 Fold and unfold.

13 Fold and unfold. Rotate.

14 Fold and unfold.

15 Fold and unfold on the
left and right. Rotate.

16 Repeat steps 14–15
five times.

17 Fold and unfold. Rotate.

18 Repeat step 17
five times.

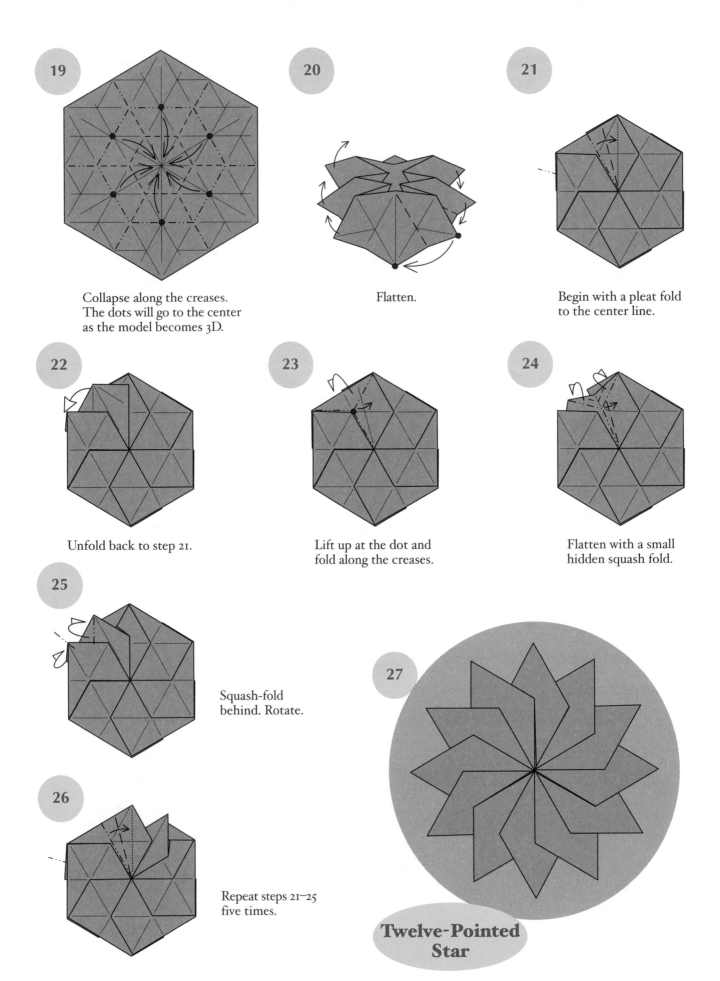

19 Collapse along the creases. The dots will go to the center as the model becomes 3D.

20 Flatten.

21 Begin with a pleat fold to the center line.

22 Unfold back to step 21.

23 Lift up at the dot and fold along the creases.

24 Flatten with a small hidden squash fold.

25 Squash-fold behind. Rotate.

26 Repeat steps 21–25 five times.

27

Twelve-Pointed Star

Colorful Twelve-Pointed Propeller

This Colorful Propeller is a beautiful but dangerous star. It has been known to slice through other stars on its journey to circle through its galaxy. Once you have captured it, handle it with care.

1

Fold and unfold.

2

Fold and unfold.

3

Fold and unfold.

4

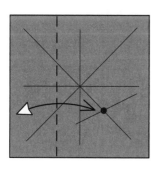

Fold and unfold.

5

Fold and unfold.

6

Fold and unfold.

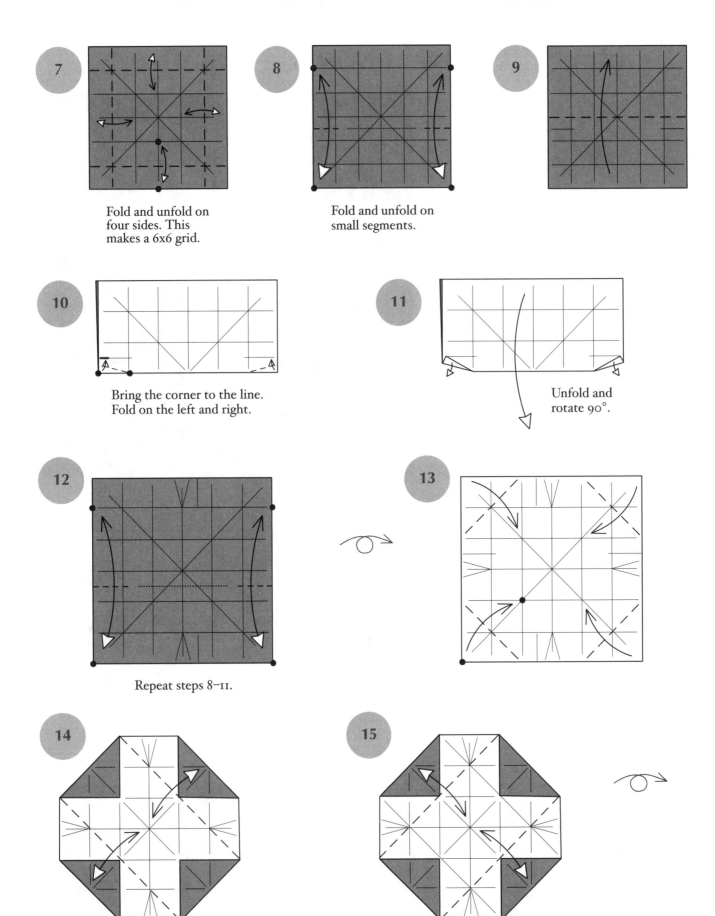

7 Fold and unfold on four sides. This makes a 6x6 grid.

8 Fold and unfold on small segments.

9

10 Bring the corner to the line. Fold on the left and right.

11 Unfold and rotate 90°.

12 Repeat steps 8–11.

13

14 Fold and unfold.

15 Fold and unfold. Rotate.

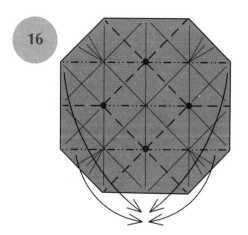

Push in at the dots and
fold along the creases.

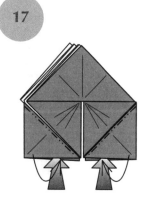

Reverse folds.

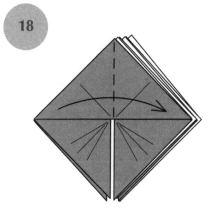

Fold one layer.

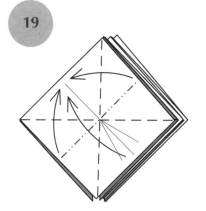

This is similar to the
waterbomb base.

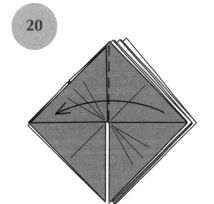

Repeat steps 18–19
on the right.

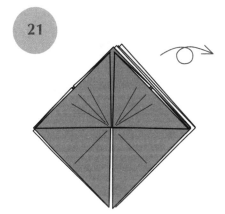

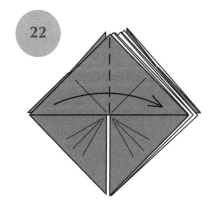

Repeat steps 18–20.

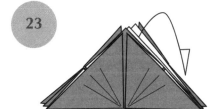

Unfold from behind.

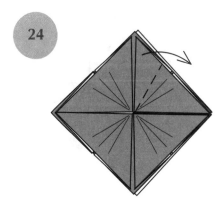

Fold along the crease.

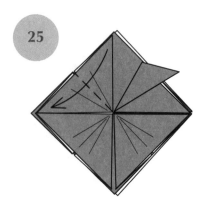

25

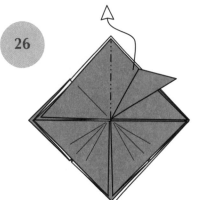

26

Pull out and lift up.

27

1. Fold to the crease, shown by the angle bisector.
2. The dots will meet. Rotate 90°.

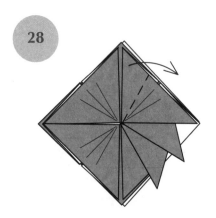

28

Repeat steps 24–27 three times.

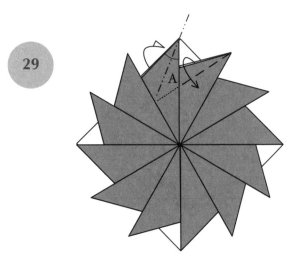

29

Squash-fold. Part of the squash fold is hidden behind region A.

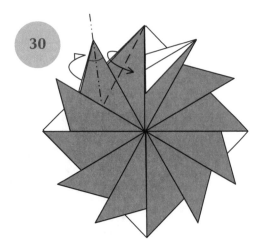

30

Repeat step 29 eleven times.

31

Rotate.

Ten and Twelve-Pointed Stars

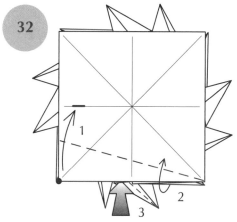

32

1. Bring the corner to the line while
2. folding all the layers together and
3. making a squash fold.
Rotate 90°.

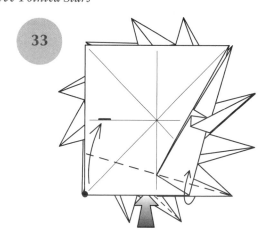

33

Repeat step 32 three times.

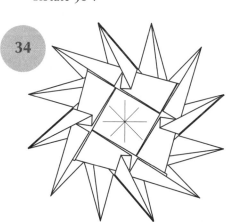

34

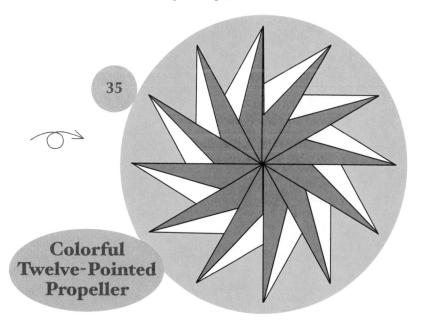

35

**Colorful
Twelve-Pointed
Propeller**

Twelve-Pointed Propeller

This Propeller will give you a ride to all the galaxies present and past. Once you have captured it with all the others, you will become the Master of the Universe. All the stars will greet you whenever you wish and will grant you radiant energy. Life-forms from all the planets will sing to you, offer their finest foods, and present you with their origami stars.

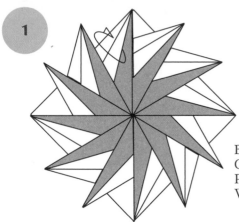

1

Begin with step 31 of the Colorful Twelve-Pointed Propeller on page 123. Wrap around.

2

Repeat step 1 eleven times.

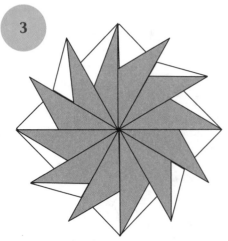

3

Continue with steps 31 to the end of the Colorful Twelve-Pointed Propeller.

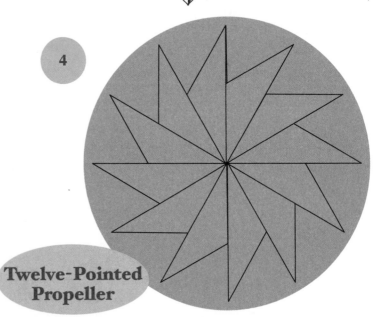

4

Twelve-Pointed Propeller